"If you look deep inside trust, you will find truth."

– *Jeffrey Gitomer*

Who do you trust?

Why do you trust them?

Who trusts you?

Why do they trust you?

How do you gain trust?

How do you become trusted?

How do you lose trust?

Why do you lose it?

Can you regain lost trust?

How important is trust in
your business relationships?

How important is trust in
your personal relationships?

The answers are inside this book...

Jeffrey Gitomer's

LITTLE TEAL BOOK *of*

TRUST

3 1336 08616 3780

*How to Earn it, Grow it,
and Keep it to Become a*

TRUSTED ADVISOR
in Sales, Business, & Life

FT Press
FINANCIAL TIMES

The Little Teal Book of Trust

© 2008 Pearson Education, Inc. Publishing as FT Press
Upper Saddle River, New Jersey 07458.
Vice President and Editor-in-Chief: Tim Moore.

The Little Book Series is a registered trademark of Jeffrey Gitomer.

To order additional copies of this title, contact your local bookseller or call
704/333-1112.

The author may be contacted at the following address:
BuyGitomer
310 Arlington Ave., Loft 329
Charlotte, NC 28203
Phone: 704/333-1112 Fax: 704/333-1011
E-mail: salesman@gitomer.com
Web sites: www.gitomer.com, www.trainone.com

Creative Director: Jessica McDougall
Pagesetting: Michael Wolff
Proofreading: Nate Pritts and Claudia Wolff
Cover design: Josh Gitomer

Printed in China by RR Donnelley.

First Printing, November 2008

Library of Congress Cataloging-in-Publication Data

Gitomer, Jeffrey H.
  Jeffrey Gitomer's little teal book of trust : how to earn it, grow it,
and keep it to become a trusted advisor in sales, business, and life /
Jeffrey Gitomer.
      p. cm.
  ISBN 0-13-715410-0 (hardback : alk. paper)
  1. Customer relations. 2. Trust. 3. Organizational behavior. 4.
Interpersonal relations. I. Title. II. Title: Little teal book of trust
: how to earn it, grow it, and keep it to become a trusted advisor in
sales, business, and life.
  HF5415.5.G544 2008
  158.2--dc22
                                                      2008032963

TRUST ME!

The words "Trust me" have been uttered billions of times –
and every time those words are spoken, it's because the
other person doesn't.

Trust is not a request.
Trust is earned.

Trust is not spoken.
Trust is a feeling.

The reason trust is requested is because the person
seeking trust realizes that "trust" is the key to "yes."

Think about the times you requested someone's trust.
It might have been something simple like choosing a
restaurant or a movie. Maybe it was a customer in a sales
presentation, or something bigger like a real estate deal.
Maybe it was a big decision that you wanted to be made
in your favor. Because no one was in instant agreement
with you, and you felt that your way was the best way or
that your idea was the best idea, you immediately asked
someone (or a group of people) to trust you.

"Trust me on this one."

Their response to your request for trust was in large part based on how much they trusted you to begin with. If you knew everyone and had a past history of success, it's more likely that people would have gone along. If you had no history with them, or only a checkered one, it's likely you would have been met with resistance.

The fulcrum point is based around the word and the feeling of trust. You may ask for it, but if the other person doesn't feel it, you're not going to get it.

"I trusted you right up until the moment you said 'trust me'!"

"The reason
you have to say
'Trust me!' is that
you haven't earned
it and are forced
to ask for it – bad
move."

– *Jeffrey Gitomer*

Why should I trust you?

Because of a background growing up in the Northeast, trust was an elusive element in many of my dealings. I didn't realize it at the time. I certainly didn't realize its importance. I just thought that lack of trust was a way of life, not a missing element. As I matured and developed relationships and finally moved away, I realized that trust was not AN important element, it was THE important element in building long-term success with anyone or any company.

The answer to "Why should I trust you?" is a simple one. Trust will allow two people to reach virtually any level in a relationship. The greater the trust factor, the more expansive the relationship can become.

Where trust does not exist, the potential for a relationship remains in the transactional area. Buy and sell. Or service and leave – nothing beyond the face value of the situation.

The secret, and it's not a big one, is to become trustworthy. You accomplish this over a period of time with words, actions, and deeds that allow trust to be built.

The more trustworthy you become, the more success you have the potential to achieve. Not just in a single relationship, but in any endeavor you undertake.

Here are the reasons I want to trust you:

- I want to trust you because I want to believe what you have told me is true.

- I want to trust you because I've just given you my money, and I want to know that it is safe.

- I want to trust you because I've just given you my money, and I want to know that you'll deliver what I've been promised.

- I want to trust you because I've just confided something in you.

- I want to trust you because I've just asked you to do something for me, and it's important that it gets done in a timely manner.

- I want to trust you because I've just asked you to do something for me, and I want it to be the best it possibly can be.

- I want to trust you because I've just asked for your advice and I want you to tell me what's in my best interest...not what's in your best interest.

- I want to trust you because I love you.

- I want to trust you because you've given me your word and I'm assuming it's your bond.

What is this book about?

As stated on the cover, trust is the theme of this book. However, this book is also about what makes trust happen, how trust occurs, how to trust, how you become trustworthy, and everything in between including the downside: how you lose trust, and what those ramifications are.

The benefit you will derive from this book has trust as an outcome, and the elements of the book are what will lead you to that reward.

These are the elements that, when mastered, manifest themselves in trust:

- **Relationships**
- **Judgment**
- **Truth**
- **Value**
- **Servant**
- **Giving trust**
- **Getting trust**

Once these elements have been explained and you have a firm understanding of their role in the trust factor, then the book evolves to a higher level called *trusted advisor* – a status that everyone seeks to have.

It's a status that all bosses tell their salespeople to become, a status that every professional (doctor, lawyer, accountant) seeks to achieve, and a status that everyone either silently or vocally aspires to.

I try to write to be understood. I'm known for, and have built a reputation on, simplistic, straightforward information that you can use one minute after you read it.

This book is different.

The information is still straightforward. And I believe it to be easily understood. But trust is not instant. And earning the rank of trusted advisor is less instant than that.

This is a book that will service you for a lifetime of growth and a lifetime of success as you seek to understand and master the principles of trust and become a trustworthy person.

About now you may be asking yourself *Is this a business book? A sales book? Or a personal development book?*

The answer to all three questions is  **YES!**

Trust forms the foundation
for everything you do in
business, and everything you
do in your personal life.

Think about who you do business with. Think about all the products that you buy. Think about all the people you interact with in your daily life. Think about members of your family. Your trust for them and in them, and their trust in you, create the opportunity for all other aspects of your friendships and relationships to mature, expand, and blossom.

I don't have to stress the importance of trust. You already know it. What I intend to stress are the elements that make trust happen and the incidents that make it disappear.

This is not a book that fits in one pigeon hole or another, and it's not a book to be read by only salespeople or only customer service people – this is a book to be read and studied by everyone who thinks trust is important to gain, more important to keep, and most important to honor. You included.

Table of Contents

SECTION 3: 23.5 CHARACTERISTICS OF TRUSTED AND TRUSTWORTHY PEOPLE

SECTION 4: BUSINESS AND SALES ADVICE YOU CAN TRUST...AND BANK ON

SECTION 5: TRUST RECOVERY

SECTION 6: BECOMING A TRUSTED ADVISOR

SECTION 6.5: TRUTH, TRUST, VALUE

ASK YOURSELF...

"Do not trust all men, but trust men of worth; the former course is silly, the latter a mark of prudence."

– Democritus (460 BC - 370 BC)

Do you trust yourself?

Have you ever looked back at a decision you made and scolded yourself, almost punished yourself, for making the wrong decision or realizing you could have made a better decision?

Monday-morning quarterbacks are always correct. They see what could have been done or should have been done on Sunday, and talk about it Monday as though they could have gone back to Sunday and done it themselves.

People who go back and chastise themselves, or second guess themselves, for making a wrong decision or a weak decision continue to set themselves up for failure in future decisions simply because they don't trust themselves.

I maintain that your judgment should always be trusted and never be second guessed.

That doesn't mean you won't make errors. That's why they call it judgment.

But I'm challenging you to look at incorrect decisions as *lessons*, life's lessons.

Mistakes in judgment are the best teachers in the world, and if you choose to learn from them, then you will begin to trust yourself and understand that, correct or incorrect, you were decisive and moved on.

In order for you to understand the elements of this book, you must first learn to trust yourself – your judgments, your actions, and your words both spoken and written. You can't trust others until you trust yourself.

Oh, you may rely on others. Oh, you may be dependent on others. But reliance and dependence are mutually exclusive of trust.

HERE'S THE SECRET AGAIN: In order to build trust and become a trusted advisor to others, you have to first trust yourself. This means you have to trust your thinking, your wisdom, your knowledge, your judgment, your instincts, your powers of observation, your powers of deduction, your ability to reason, and your ability to discern.

You must be decisive. Trusted people are not wishy-washy. Trusted people do not pass the buck. Trusted people are willing to bet on themselves.

It's NOT "trust me."
It's TRUST YOURSELF.

"You can't trust others until you trust yourself."

– *Jeffrey Gitomer*

Why should you trust others?

Early on in my career, in spite of advice from others and my living environment, I somehow decided to give other people the initial benefit of the doubt. I became a trusting soul. I decided that I would trust everyone until they gave me, or proved to me, reasons why I should not. That philosophy was and remains very risky, especially in my present position where I have much more to lose than I did back then.

BUT, by giving others initial trust, I automatically became wide open to, and accepting of, new ideas, new thoughts, and new strategies for success.

I have found that most people do not initially trust. You see their arms folded. You feel their internal barriers built. If you're old like me, you can remember the Ipana toothpaste commercial with the invisible protective shield. People who lack that vulnerability, or people who have those barriers raised first, will overlook incredible opportunities based on initial prejudgments or even intransigence (thinking no without the possibility of yes).

ADVICE: Lower your barriers. Unfold your arms. Be vulnerable. Trust first.

I will admit to you that my philosophy of trusting initially has stung me, hurt me, and even burned me several times. But boy have I won, and won big, as a result of being vulnerable enough to trust. And I challenge you to do the same.

Why should you take someone's advice?

Taking advice is a very sensitive and delicate process because it usually means someone else has helped you make a decision or made the decision for you, and you were willing to accept it based on a combination of your gut-level feeling and your trust.

The short answer is you're not going to take someone's advice, especially financial advice or advice that could have a major impact on your life, if you don't trust or have a good feeling about the person offering the advice.

Here are the 4.5 reasons why you will take someone else's advice in order to help you make a decision:

1. You're friends with them. When you're seeking advice, or when someone is offering unsolicited advice, you'll listen closer if that person is a friend of yours.

2. You trust their expertise. They have a greater degree of knowledge than you do and you're wiling to chance trusting them in the hopes that the advice will be accurate and sound, and that the outcome will be what you're hoping for.

3. You have a relationship. This is someone that you've known for a long time – a significant other or a spouse, someone that you have grown to care about, grown to honor, grown to believe, and of course grown to trust.

4. Your immediate family. Oftentimes their advice will come in a discouraging manner. And you, like me, ignore the advice until it becomes obvious truth.

4.5 Battling logic versus emotion as you receive this advice. The advice may be logical, but your emotions prevent you from hearing it, much less taking it. The best thing to do is not make an immediate decision where high emotion is involved. Listen to others, write down the facts, the options, and the potential outcomes. Then spend quality time thinking about what's the right thing to do and the best thing to do. The decision will become obvious.

"The last person's advice I trusted was the math teacher who told me that algebra would be useful to me someday!

Are your neighbors and friends your advisors? At some level, YES!

From something as small as where to eat and what movie to see, or as major as where to take a vacation or what car to buy, your neighbors, your friends, your relatives, and your coworkers are 1,000 times more influential in your decision making process than a person trying to sell to you.

Are you going to believe your next-door neighbor who has been there, or the travel agent who has never been there? Are you going to believe your next-door neighbor, or the car salesperson? It's most likely you will believe your friends and neighbors because they have both direct experience and they're not affected by the outcome. They won't make a commission on the sale.

Whether you're buying a car or looking for a good restaurant, think about whose advice you seek, and whose advice you're willing to take. Those people you seek will not just give you advice; they give you comfort and support, and they have no personal agenda or axe to grind in giving you that advice. That's why you're skeptical of the advertisement, or why you avoid the salesperson. You seek people who you believe will tell you the truth and help confirm in your mind, or justify in your mind, that which you want to do, but need more support in doing. That's why your neighbor has more power than the ad in the paper or the car salesman.

Higher levels of trust – health, home, money

These three areas of life define your safety, your security, and your overall quality of life. Advice in regards to any major decision made in these areas has to come from someone that you trust.

If you need a heart operation, if you're looking to buy a new home or upgrade the one you have, or if you're looking to make some large investment, it's a given that you will seek out people that you trust.

Review your recent health, home, and money issues, and identify the people involved in helping you with those decisions. Then, think about the qualifications that enabled you to trust those people. Was it their expertise, their friendship, their past history of performance? Or was it all of the above combined with your gut feeling to move forward?

Whatever the criteria was, it's important that you understand it and capture it for future endeavors – but it's more important that you try to create some of those qualities and characteristics in yourself.

The best way to learn how to become trustworthy is to study other trustworthy people.

GOING BROKE IS TRUST LOST: If you've ever gone bankrupt, it stays on your record somewhere between 7 and 10 years. The world will either refuse or be reluctant to trust you for that period of time.

It means others have lost faith in your ability to take on debt or repay debt. Even though it may not have been your fault, when trust is gone, people, especially banks and credit card institutions, don't really care whose fault it is.

That gives you an idea of how long it takes to regain trust in every other aspect of your life.

*"The identity I stole was a fake!
Boy, you just can't trust people these days!"*

Do I trust my partner?

Think about the partners that you've had throughout your life, both in business and personal relationships. In the courtship stage, everything is wonderful. In a business deal, you may clarify things in a contract. In a marriage proposal, you might create a prenuptial agreement clarifying who gets what if the relationship ends.

But as a business or personal relationship matures, episodes or incidents occur that may cause you to rethink present status. When the first incident occurs, you tend to give the other person "the benefit of the doubt." Innocent until proven guilty.

Sure you may give the other person the benefit of the doubt, but the doubt will still be present. If a second or third incident occurs, benefit of the doubt may turn into confrontation. And if the violation of trust continues to take place, the relationship will begin to erode.

When trust begins to evaporate, the partnership becomes strained. And, depending on the violation, it may never get back to the same place that it once was. That's how powerful trust is.

What are the elements that lead to trustworthiness?

These elements are what has guided you to your present situation – how you trust others and who trusts you.

THE FIRST ELEMENT IS: *How you were raised.* Your family – your parents and your siblings – presented opportunities for you to react and respond to. Did you lie to them? Did you take things when no one was looking? Did you always do the right thing, or try to get away with the wrong thing? And for how many years did those actions occur? Small errors in judgment repeated over time will lead to failure.

THE SECOND ELEMENT IS: *Who you chose to associate with:* your friends, other outside family members. What kind of people were they? What were their characters like?

THE THIRD ELEMENT IS: *People of influence* – your teachers, your priest, minister, or rabbi, your heroes, or your mentor. Those people gave you advice that you either took or ignored, and that advice built your character or modified it.

The combination of those three elements and your responses over time to situations as they occur, especially in dealings of money, promises kept, or situations of honor, has built the foundation of your trustworthiness. Everyone is exposed to situations and opportunities that they can take advantage of by doing the right thing or doing the wrong thing.

You already know what the right thing is. You certainly knew what the right thing was each time an opportunity occurred. The choices that you have been exercising during your life up to this point have determined your trustworthiness to others.

Take a moment and think about the qualities of the people you consider trustworthy. You don't have to list the people. But you do have to list the qualities and characteristics. That will give you an idea of what you need to aspire to and a measuring stick as to where you are on the trustworthy scale right now.

Later in the book, I will present a detailed list of the individual characteristics that, when combined, can create an atmosphere of trust. Here I just want to clarify that all of those characteristics combine to equal your character.

It is your *character* that sits at the foundation of your ability to build trust. Your *character* eventually manifests itself into your reputation.

What you are known as.
What you are known by.
And what you are known for.

It is what people may say about your when you're not present. And it is what people might say on your behalf as a character reference or testimonial.

"Your character
holds the
key to your
trustworthiness."

— Jeffrey Gitomer

Below are characteristics of what will develop your trustworthiness. Rate yourself from 1-5 for each one.

1=never, 2=rarely, 3=sometimes, 4=frequently, 5=all the time

People rely on me.	1	2	3	4	5
When someone gives me a job to do, it's always done on or ahead of time.	1	2	3	4	5
When someone gives me a job to do, it's always done to the best of my ability.	1	2	3	4	5
I have a reputation for getting the job done no matter what.	1	2	3	4	5
I am always on time.	1	2	3	4	5
I am dependable.	1	2	3	4	5
I am honest.	1	2	3	4	5
I tell the truth all the time.	1	2	3	4	5
When people trust me with a secret, they know their secret is safe.	1	2	3	4	5
When people trust me with matters of money, they know their money is safe.	1	2	3	4	5

This test is not specifically for scoring purposes; it's more for self-awareness purposes. If your score is high, it's most likely that you're trustworthy. If your score is a bunch of 3s and 4s, you're on the edge. And if your score is a bunch of 2s and 3s – you're probably not very trustworthy.

Who do you trust?

Think about the people you trust. It's a very deep thought that must be broken down into sub-thoughts.

These are the people you would go to at your highest time of need. These are people who are able to influence you as you make life decisions.

Start with your top five people.

List them here:

1. _____

2. _____

3. _____

4. _____

5. _____

I'll bet that as you were thinking of people, several reasons, maybe even several memories, flashed across your mind.

The justification for why you may have had a hard time filling in the list is that no one has ever asked you to come up with this list before.

You're having to think very deeply about a very profound element of your life – the element of trust.

For the most part, the people on your list will be people that you have known for a long time – friends or relatives who have proven themselves time and again to be worthy of your trust.

Their consistent actions, especially in times of need, have earned them a position of being trustworthy in your life.

WORD OF CAUTION: You may trust people's wisdom or specific knowledge, but not trust the person. For example, you may trust your computer guy to fix your computer, but you may not trust his judgment to help you make a financial decision about a piece of land that you're going to buy. The computer guy has what is known as competency trust. His expertise is way beyond your expertise, and you accept his judgment or wisdom; you trust his information and advice to be valid and accurate. The same competency trust may be present in your dentist, your doctor, your lawyer, your auto repairman, or your landscaper. You trust them – but only for their information, not necessarily as a person.

Now let's get back to those that you trust as people – the ones in your inner circle. You don't just accept their wisdom on a specific topic; you accept and respect their advice on a multitude of topics.

The people you trust are the people that you "bounce things off of." They're the ones whose reasoning you accept – whose value judgments are so powerful that they can alter your existing feelings or desires. But it's more powerful to understand how they got to this position, and how they earned this level of trust in your mind.

Here are a few reasons why you trust them:

1. You believe they have your best interest at heart.

2. You believe they have no "agenda" and no axe to grind. In other words, they're not giving you advice based on what's good for them. They're giving you advice based on what's good for you.

3. Money is not a motive in your relationship and is not an influencer in the way they guide you.

4. You have a past history of friendship.

5. You have a past history of successful exchanges.

6. You believe that what they're telling you is the truth – all the time.

6.5 There's an unspoken good feeling when you're with them or when you're speaking to them. You have a very high level of comfort. You have a private, verbal intimacy that gives you peace and peace of mind.

Go back and look at your list of trusted people.

Next to each person, put a dash followed by three qualities that they possess that have created your trust in them.

Who trusts you?

Everyone wants to be trusted, and everyone wants to believe that they're trustworthy. Let's go through the list process again – only this time let's create one list that includes the people who trust YOU because of your specific knowledge, and another list for the people who trust you as a person.

These are the people who rely on me for my specific knowledge or my specific expertise in my chosen field of endeavor (whether it's accounting, sales, or fixing air conditioners):

1. _____
2. _____
3. _____
4. _____
5. _____

These are the people who rely on me for help, for support, and for wisdom about life:

1. _____
2. _____
3. _____
4. _____
5. _____

If you're in business or in sales, you want your customers to trust you enough to continue to do business with you. If you're a doctor, or a lawyer, or an accountant, you want your customers (also erroneously referred to as clients or patients) to trust you enough to take your advice and continue to do business with you. That's a solid level of trust on the "trust me scale."

The easiest way to begin to understand how and why others trust you is by gauging the questions they ask you. If the questions are always about your specific knowledge, the level of trust will always be centered around your expertise. The more the questions get personal, the higher their level of trust will evolve.

But either way, trust at any level requires the same basic elements – truth, sincerity, perceived value, past history of success, and the other person's confidence in you as a person to say okay and move forward. The more others trust you, the faster you will get from point A to point B.

For example, if you need a new computer with specific storage capacity and performance requirements, you may call three or four people and "shop around" until you find what you believe that you need.

Not me. I call Tommy Berry. He's my computer guy. He knows my company, he knows my systems, and he knows me personally. For almost 20 years, he has been my computer go-to guy. I call him on the phone, I tell him what I need, and, in a day or two, something appears. And for the past 20 years, that has worked. Not only for me, but also for Tommy.

Everyone in my company trusts Tommy Berry's judgment and takes his advice freely. The only problem we've had with Tommy is that we wish he were always there to answer every computer problem or situation instantly. That's only a problem for us. And, by the way, Tommy . Berry and I are also friends.

I'll quote a phrase I have used in several of my books...

"All things being equal, people want to do business with their friends. All things being not quite so equal, people still want to do business with their friends."

Tommy's likeability combined with his expertise about computers and his knowledge of my business gives him a green light and an acceptance to provide products and services. In short, I trust Tommy.

Hopefully that short vignette will give you some insight as to why people may or may not trust you. Business people, especially salespeople, seek to gain trust right away when in fact trust is far away in a new relationship.

HERE'S THE SECRET: First comes likeability. Then comes believability. Then comes confidence. And finally, trust begins to emerge. Slowly.

If you're looking for the elements of those who trust you, they are the same reasons that I trust Tommy. I like him, I believe him, I have confidence in him, and over an extended period of time he has proven himself to be both accurate and valuable. Trustworthy.

As you move forward in this book, every page that's written contains ideas and examples, thoughts and strategies, and wisdom and insights for you to become more trustworthy, for you to become more trusted, and for you to become a more valued resource to those with whom you seek to build a relationship.

But, more important, there's a personal side to trust and who trusts you. The relationship side. The family side. Mother. Father. Husband. Wife. Child. Everyone talks about love and love of family. Very few ever talk about trust. In my opinion, the more you have trust in the other person, the more you have faith in the other person – the more capable and the more probable it is that love is being exchanged. And that the other person will trust you.

Who trusts who?

Everyone, including you, makes a value judgment based on what they know and who they know. At the top of the value judgment list is trust.

And once you understand trust as it relates to you, and you see the potential power that it has in building your relationships and your future – not just in success, but in fulfillment – the hunger for knowledge to become more trustworthy, more trustable, and more trust giving will become a priority.

"Never trust anyone over 30 inches!"

"If you don't give trust to others, it's because they haven't earned it. If you don't have trust from others, it's because YOU haven't earned it."

— *Jeffrey Gitomer*

What is the image you have of yourself?

How do you picture yourself?

Pretty powerful question when you think about it.

TELL ME ABOUT THE PICTURE: Is it a physical picture (tall, pretty) or a mental picture (self-assured, confident)? Is it a positive picture (great attitude, successful) or a negative picture (failing, in debt)? Did you picture the "now" or "what you want to become?"

Some of you are thinking handsome or pretty, some overweight or average, some successful or struggling. Some pictures are happy; some are not – very not!

Almost none of you will put trustworthy or untrustworthy.

Even less of you will put honest or dishonest.

And none of you will put truthful or liar.

What I have found interesting about picturing yourself is that most people don't want to look. They don't like what they see or they don't like themselves. And then there's that ever-present, unavoidable bathroom mirror.

Suppose I told you that the more vivid the picture, the more accepting you'll be of yourself and the more you can see that tomorrow is the fast track to success. Would you at least take a peek?

FIRST TRUTH – TRUST YOURSELF: The picture you have of yourself, combined with the self-belief that goes with it, is what, and who, you are likely to become.

If you look at (read) some of the books written on the subject of self-image and visualization, you'll be surprised to find that they all have a common theme: *The easiest way to get where you want to go is to picture yourself there in advance.*

The breakthrough book *Psycho-Cybernetics* by Dr. Maxwell Maltz, is the classic example of what self-image is about. I read the book back in the early 1970s and often read a few pages as part of my commitment to lifelong learning.

Maltz says, "We react to the image we have of ourselves in our brain. Change that image for the better and our lives improve. Self-image is changed for the better or worse not by intellect alone, not by intellectual knowledge alone, but by experiencing."

This goes for any aspect of your life.

If you want success...

If you want wealth...

If you want a new home...

If you want to become a doctor...

If you want to win the game...

If you want to climb the mountain...

If you want to run a marathon...

If you want to become a great dad or mom...

If you want to make that big sale...

First picture yourself already doing it – or having achieved it.

SECOND TRUTH – TRUST YOUR BELIEFS: You are in complete control of the beliefs and pictures that you put in your head.

Not only are you in total control of your mind, you can also alter (control) your environment to enhance that control. Where you are can affect the way you think.

HERE'S A DEEPER THOUGHT: If you don't like your job or boss, it will be extremely difficult for you to have the positive mental picture necessary for achievement. You gotta love what you do (or at least like it a lot)! How can you visualize success in a job you don't like or when you work for someone you don't trust or admire?

Answer: You can't!

THIRD TRUTH – TRUST YOUR THOUGHTS: If you change your self-image in your mind, you will begin to achieve a mental image and live your thoughts.

In her book, *Creative Visualization,* Shakti Gawain says, "Imagination is the ability to create an idea, a mental picture, or a feeling or sense of something. In creative visualization you use your imagination to create a clear image, idea, or feeling of something you wish to manifest.

Then you continue to focus on the idea, feeling, or picture regularly, giving it positive energy until it becomes objective reality ... in other words, until you actually achieve what you have been imagining."

These two wisdom-filled books, *Psycho-Cybernetics* and *Creative Visualization*, are books you may want to add to your library as you seek to improve your self-image, build stronger self-belief, eliminate self-limitations, and block self-defeating thoughts. Just a thought.

"But Jeffrey," you ask, "can I do all of this just by reading?"

Heck no! This is not about simply thinking or visualizing. That's just the beginning. You still have to TAKE ACTION to make it happen.

HERE'S THE SECRET: Committed, passionate self-belief leads to action – achievement action. Action (with a dash of passion and positive anticipation) leads to results. And those results will be your vision fulfilled.

"The only way to achieve your desires and dreams is to ACT ON THEM. The greater you trust in yourself, your beliefs, and your thoughts, the more action you will take."

– Jeffrey Gitomer

Honesty…
a self-assessment

The easiest person to be dishonest with is yourself. The reason is, like everyone, you justify your dishonesty in one manner or another. Hundreds of thousands of workers steal from their employers with the justification that, because they're underpaid, the company owes it to them, and the company won't miss it anyway because they have plenty of money.

I'm drawing a fine line here between honesty and truth. Truth being more word-oriented. Honesty being more deed-oriented.

Being honest when you're dealing with others is easier to do because your honesty is on the table for all to view.

Being honest with yourself is more difficult because you only have to justify it in private where no one can see it.

It's like trying to quit smoking, but having a cigarette when no one's looking. Milder versions might be cheating on your diet or on a test at school.

It seems as though honesty has taken a left turn in sales. When a manager demands that a salesperson make at least 20 cold calls a week and it's Sunday night and you're filling out your sales report and you made only 13 calls, somehow the number 21 will find its way onto your report. The word honesty is a more powerful word than the words truth or lie. The words "Honest Abe" are more powerful than the words "Truthful Abe." However, dishonesty will almost always manifest itself as a lie rather than a dishonest action.

Becoming honest with yourself takes a hell of a lot of courage – because it means doing the right thing when no one's looking. There's pride in honesty. There's pride in being honorable. People who are honest with themselves are more trustworthy people than their counterparts. And they're the people you trust in times of need because you know they'll do the right thing by you, because they always do the right thing by themselves.

Here are 3.5 things you can do that will make you, or even force you, to become more honest with yourself:

1. Find an honest partner and exchange moments of truth. Discuss aspects of dishonesty and how you might have done better in the past and how you plan to correct that and be better in the future.

2. Don't give in to yourself when no one's looking. Pass on the cigarette. Pass on the beer. Pass on the donut. You know the old adage is "You're only hurting yourself," but the fact is it doesn't hurt so bad at that moment, and so you take the path of least resistance. Don't do it!

3. Tell the truth when a lie would do and no one would ever know. Tell your boss you made only 13 cold calls. Tell your mother what you omitted from the actions that you took.

3.5 As painful as this might be, go back to your recent past and make a list of times when you were dishonest. It might have been cheating on a test in school, cheating on a game that you played, taking something that didn't belong to you, or bumping into someone's car in a parking lot and leaving the scene. List the things that you "got away with," things that in retrospect were not that big of a deal, but at the time were easy to avoid. Maybe make a phone call or two, and a confession or three. Or simply resolve to yourself that it won't happen again, and move forward.

> A big part of honesty is self-discipline, personal resolve, and taking pride in who you are as a person and what each action means to your character.

THE SIMPLE FORMULA IS: If it doesn't make you proud, or it's not something that you would brag about to your mother, it's probably something you could do a better way, a more honorable way, and a more honest way. Do that.

The 14.5
definitions
of trust

"Self-trust is the first secret of success."

– Ralph Waldo Emerson

The 14.5 definitions of trust

1. The risk of trust and trusting – trust is a risk. Trust is risky, especially when you're giving it to someone else.

Have you ever trusted someone only to have them violate your trust? You felt used, burned, angered, and basically crossed that person off of your list forever. Oh, you may still talk to them. You may even be friendly to that person. But once trust has been violated, it's not likely to return.

That's the risk you take when you trust. The easiest examples to give are when a loan doesn't get paid back, a secret gets retold to others, a confidence gets broken, or a promise goes unfulfilled. You risked giving someone trust, and the risk was not rewarded. In fact, the risk was violated. That's the negative side.

If you think back in your life, you'll probably find that the ratio of trust fulfilled versus trust unfulfilled is more than 10 to 1 in favor of trust rewarded. Like anything else in life, the associated risk carries with it a potential for hurt.

The reason I begin defining trust as risk is because all the other definitions carry some form of risk with them. If you've read my previous books, you know my feeling about risk. The old saying is "No risk, no reward." My saying is "No risk, no nothing."

Risk of Secrets. Trusting someone else with the truth is a big risk. Should I trust you with my secret? Virtually no one can keep a secret. There's an old Benjamin Franklin quote that goes, "Two can keep a secret if one is dead." And that quote is pretty close to the truth.

Risk of Confidentiality. You're probably familiar with the word *leak*. For example, someone in politics leaked something to the press in direct violation of the confidence which he was entrusted. I don't know how you define that type of action. I refer to it as low-life, certainly not something you'd want to teach your children. But it's a classic example of someone else's confidence compromised or violated. And worse, the person who did it doesn't even have the guts to come forward. Reason – they might go to jail. The good news is some of them do.

Who has violated your confidence? Whether it's a stock tip, or a product launch, or a new fashion design, or an upcoming pregnancy or marriage, or even something as simple as a surprise party, someone decided to take your confidence and betray it. Hopefully those inappropriate actions will serve as a negative benchmark for you not to be that type of person.

If you ever get a chance to watch old Sherlock Holmes movies with Basil Rathbone as Sherlock Holmes and Nigel Bruce as Dr. Watson, you'll see that when a client comes to Sherlock Holmes and questions his ability to keep the matter confidential, his pat response is, "I assure you, I am the very soul of discretion."

I wonder if you can make that statement?

Risk of Money. Have you ever loaned money to someone and not been paid back? Of course you have. Everyone has. The opposite of that is have you ever borrowed money from someone and not paid them back? The bottom line is issues of money involve both risk and disappointment. My dad taught me not to lend money. He said, "Son, just give it away. You probably won't get it back anyway. And this way, you won't be disappointed." I recommend you do the same. If you cannot afford to lend the money, don't. It's better to say no and risk losing the friend than it is to say yes, not be repaid, and lose the friend.

In all of these three risk elements – secrets, confidentiality, and money – trust is at the fulcrum point. If you don't trust, you won't tell the secret, you won't share the message, you won't lend the money. And if you do trust, there's still a risk.

Everyone has what is known as risk tolerance. It will determine whether you're willing to risk or not, or how much you're willing to risk.

People go to Las Vegas and set aside an amount of money that they can tolerate risking or losing. Most of them lose it. And some lose more than they can afford. The city of Las Vegas is counting on that. That's how all the hotels get built. But you have a tolerance for risk that you should come to grips with so that you can understand things like when to change jobs, when to make an investment, when to buy a house and, these days, when to trade the car. Your tolerance ties back to the risk of trusting. Take some time to identify yours, and you'll be able to make better, stronger judgments.

2. Initial trust is tentative. Picture this. You're on the beach for vacation. You run down to the oceanfront and put one toe in the water. The old expression is "testing the waters." You don't want to risk the water being too cold or too rough, so you just go in a little bit, and then a little more – and now you're up to your waist. And finally, after jumping around and becoming accustomed to the water, you dive in. It's the same in any other issue in your life; the only difference is, there's no water. You trust people a little bit at a time until you become comfortable, and then you're willing to make some kind of a deal. Now that you understand that about yourself, you may understand why other people are somewhat hesitant to trust you. They're testing you. They want to feel safe. They want to become accustomed to you. And then they'll dive in.

"Why can't you trust me? If I was fooling around with your wife, don't you think you'd notice?"

3. Trust is a form of faith. Take out a United States dollar bill or a coin. Upon close inspection, you'll find the four words "IN GOD WE TRUST." That phrase is on every piece of U.S. coin and currency and has been in whole or in part since the 1850s. American citizens have faith in the country and faith in the currency. You may look at faith as something to take part in on Saturday or Sunday at a church or synagogue. That's only one small part of faith. Trust is a form of faith in that you have to believe in what you're doing and who you're doing it with. In short, you have to have faith in them. I personally believe that faith precedes trust. You have faith in yourself, you believe in yourself; you have faith in others, you believe in others – and then you begin to trust. When trust is present, then you're willing to take a risk.

4. Trust lowers resistance. People resist moving forward based on their present judgment of the situation that's occurring now. They're making a self-judgment as well as a transferred judgment. If you've ever heard someone say, "I don't trust my own judgment," what it means is the person can't make up his mind, or is not a very decisive person. The late, great Charles Schulz defined it best when Lucy referred to Charlie Brown as "wishy washy." If people trust their own judgment, then clearly their tolerance for trust in you is uncomfortable enough for them to move ahead. It's easiest to define in sales when a customer is considering several different sources, and you cannot understand why they haven't selected you. They haven't made a judgment yet, and until they do they will make you jump through hoops. Each time you jump, you expose yourself to more judgment. And if yours is best, eventually the resistance will be lessened until finally they make a choice. More choices are based on trust than price.

5. Trust lowers barriers. When there's a stone wall between you and other people, you cannot look at the barrier as the problem. You have to look at it as a symptom. Once you discover why that symptom is there, you'll get closer to trust if you're able to lower it or deal with it in some way. Whether it's people you're interacting with or some product you're considering purchasing, the barrier that's in front of you or between you has the word trust (or the lack of it) written all over it.

In sales, barriers are mistakenly called objections. A prospective customer will say, "Your price is too high" or "I'm happy with my present supplier" or "We're not currently accepting new vendors." What they're really saying is "I trust someone else more than I trust you." Even in the case of lowest price, they trust that lowest price enough to make the purchase. If you ever get a call that says, "Can you match this price?" that means your prospective customer does not trust the other lowest price and would prefer to do business with you.

And, like a fool, you try to match the other person's price thereby giving away all of your profit to a customer who wants to place an order.

6. Friendship leads to trust. For years, I have espoused the saying, "All things being equal, people want to do business with their friends. All things being not quite so equal, people still want to do business with their friends." I have told many unfriendly service people that it costs no extra money to be friendly. All of those pale by comparison to the trust factor. Can you imagine trusting someone who you're not in some way friendly with? Personally, I cannot. If I ask you to think about who the three people in your inner circle are that you trust the most, I guarantee you that you either like them, or love them, and that you're friends with all of them. Salespeople at low levels are told to "be professional." To me, the definition of professional is somewhere between unfriendly and downright unfriendly. Professional people get upset when you try to be friendly or inject some kind of humor. Avoid these people.

> I believe that friendly is a huge brick in the foundation of building trust, and when I seek relationships with any kind of person, I want them to err on the side of friendly.

I can't imagine trusting a grumpy person. I might consider trusting a professional person, but the barrier for trust is lowered when I interact with a friendly person. *How friendly are you?*

7. Business relationships lead to trust. Think about your top 10 customers or your top 10 business relationships.

If you're in sales, hopefully those two categories are the same. How much do they trust you? If your answer is "lots" or "they trust me implicitly," I wonder if you can go back and tell me on which day that implicit trust began. The answer is, you cannot – because trust evolves. You make a promise, and you deliver. The customer needs an order delivered a certain way at a certain time, and it's done to perfection. The customer needs service, and you're right there to perform it beyond expectation. The customer calls needing help, and you provide the help. The customer calls after hours, and you respond in five minutes.

THE KEY IS THIS: Each one of these elements builds the relationship. Each one of these actions builds trust slowly over time. Your reputation develops as reliable or dependable or as a person of service. But any one of the actions that I just described will not build trust alone. Each can build credibility – and repeated credible acts (sometimes incredible acts) lead to trust. *How credible are you? How incredible are you?*

8. Business deals are based on trust. Sales and business deals are not necessarily the same. A business deal is a higher-level sale or a higher-level agreement – a joint venture to buy or develop a property, the formation of a company, or deals that require a huge amount of trust. Business deals stem from believability, confidence, and value perception. The entrepreneur or C-level executive may ask, "Does it make sense to move forward?"

The numbers may look good. That's the logic side. But the emotional side is what drives the deal.

How believable do I perceive the other people to be? How much confidence do I have that the people and the deal will come together to be successful and profitable? What do I believe the value of this deal is to me and to others?

Once I create those mental answers, then I look at all the other people involved and ask myself, *"Do I trust these people?"* and *"How certain am I that they are truthful, credible, honorable?"* And if I believe it, what do others think? What's their reputation?

Look at your last three or four deals. Analyze them as to how trust evolved or how trust came into the picture. That analysis will help you solidify your next 100 deals.

CAUTION: There's a "greed factor." It's said that all TV commercials are based on fear, greed, and vanity. That's the motive by which the message is delivered. The classic infomercials are all based on how much money you will make if you just send yours in immediately – whether it's a real estate deal, or a day trade, or some business scheme that is sure to make you wealthy. Making money and saving money are an integral and compelling element in creating that message. Greed will block logical thinking and decision making, and greed is a higher emotion than trust. Every single person knows the phrase, "If it sounds too good to be true, it probably is," yet tens of millions of people ignore that sound advice and greedily move forward blindly. Or should I say *blinded by their ambition for money.*

9. Dealings over time lead to trust. You try out a new dry cleaner because the old one kept losing buttons. They do a pretty good job on the first bunch of clothes you bring in. So you decide to try another and another. Then you bring them things that are more delicate and more expensive. And one day they remember your name.

Slowly over time your trust in them develops. And eventually a friendship/relationship blossoms that can last for years even if there's a slip up or two.

The example I gave is one that each of you has been through. But it's no different with your family doctor, your accountant, your lawyer, your hairdresser, or anyone else that you've dealt with reliably and consistently over time.

The danger is complacency and believing that someone is doing his or her best when he or she is not. And the kicker is that someone right across the street, just around the corner, or even down the hall could do better.

My preference is to maintain loyal relationships by challenging quality at every turn. I'm not always looking for fast response, but I am always looking for best response.

10. Sales are based on trust. As you read through my other books, there are several common threads – value, differentiation, friendliness, believability, enthusiasm, and quality. If all of those elements are present in a sales presentation, then it's possible to earn trust. Once trust has been gained, a buying atmosphere is present, and it is up to the salesperson to make sure the interaction comes to a successful conclusion. You may know it as closing the sale. That's not how I look at it. I look at it as the beginning (or the continuation) of a relationship. People who trust one another don't have to close a sale. Rather, they mutually agree, each believing that the value to make it happen is present.

The easiest way for a salesperson to look at any given sales situation is to ask, "Is there a FIT? Does my product or service fit my customer's needs and ability to pay?" If the fit is there, comfort, trust, and purchase are sure to follow.

There's also the YOU DON'T UNDERSTAND factor. Imagine two companies selling the same product and one salesman saying, "You don't understand. My competition lowers the price to get the business." To that I reply, "No, YOU don't understand. Your relationship, your trust factor with the customer, was vulnerable and they decided to go with price rather than best."

"The percentage of sales that you close are in direct proportion to the degree of trust that you gain."

– Jeffrey Gitomer

11. Trust is the link between yes and no. Until trust is gained from another person, that person's answer to whatever you want will be no. Everything you're trying to persuade another person to do won't move forward until trust, or some form of trust, has been gained.

It can be as simple as making an appointment or asking someone out on a date. The degree of trust will determine the degree of YES! The higher the value of what's being offered, the higher the trust factor must be. A $10 million dollar deal or a hand in marriage both require ultimate trust.

12. Trust is a green light. Gaining trust does not mean you have crossed the finish line, but it does mean that you have permission to move forward at a significant rate of speed that will not be constantly questioned as to its validity or value. A green light does not just flash. The only light that flashes is yellow. Yellow is a cautionary light.

A green light means that you can deliver more information and that your information will be positively received. The challenge for you as a trusted person is to make certain that the information has both value and meaningful application to the recipient.

13. Personal relationships lead to trust. Think about the people you trust in your real life (as opposed to your business life): your friends, your family, your spouse or significant other. How did that trust evolve?

Especially with respect to family and spouse or significant other, what violations of trust have occurred, and how long did it take you to regain that trust, if ever?

You build relationships over an extended period of time and, in a heartbeat, based on an inappropriate action or untruth or both, trust is broken and the relationship suffers or even ends.

I have maintained that the best places to learn about attitude, loyalty, trust, and truth are at home. Those are the people who mean the most to you, and interestingly, it's also where the most violations occur.

> When people consummate a marriage, they say, "In sickness and in health," and "For better or for worse." They omit "Telling the truth" and "Trusting." Why?

Study those friendships and relationships where trust is solid, where trust is given blindly. Don't just think about them. Write down the characteristics that make those relationships solid. The most solid ones have evolved over time and are based on dependability, reliability, and truth. But I want you to discover that for yourself.

Once you've done that, create a way to apply those principles to people that you seek trust from. The obvious insight is that trust is an end result, not a beginning.

14. Marriage is based on love and trust. (This is a very sensitive subject because no matter what I say, someone will disagree with me.) I covered my basic thoughts in the relationship section, but I wanted to single out trust in marriage because people enter into it idealistically and in love. Yet over time, in more than 50% of them, love erodes, fades, or dies, and some kind of fight ensues as to who gets the television and who gets the house. Meanwhile, children suffer.

I'm certainly not a PhD in relationships, nor am I a psychologist. But I can tell you my experience over time. When trust goes, the relationship goes. And in spite of heroic efforts, it rarely returns.

14.5 Trust breeds confidence – in yourself and from others.
Confidence has three elements: 1) personal self-confidence; 2) the confidence you give others; and 3) the confidence they give you. Personal self-confidence comes from all kinds of things, including environment and associations. But to me the main element of confidence is knowing what kind of person you are and acting on that. Do you keep your word? Do you get the job done? Are you reliable, dependable, honest, forthright, self-starting, and (of course) trustworthy? Your self-confidence is the basis from which that feeling is transferred to others. And, obviously, the more success you have, the more past history of success you have, the easier it is for you to transfer that confidence to others.

Most people are skeptical. It's important to remember that as you talk, and as you act – other people are judging you at the same time you're judging them!

Their judgment is in direct proportion to their willingness to trust you.

Quoting my first rule, "Do they like you? Do they believe you? Do they have confidence in you? Do they trust you?" It's most interesting to note that the answers to those questions are within your control. If you understand that you're entering some kind of relationship, deal, or sale with a positive outcome in mind, it's much easier to gain their confidence and trust.

There's also a .5. The .5 in the confidence element is reputation. You have a reputation. And the person or the people you're dealing with have a reputation. Maybe part of that reputation comes from your past dealings with them. Even if the situation is ideal, reputation (past history) can preclude confidence and trust.

Take a moment and look at your own life. There are people in it that you absolutely trust and people that you absolutely DO NOT trust. If you make a list of the reasons that you're willing to give trust and the reasons that you're not willing to give trust, you will have at once uncovered your own trust parameters. For example, if you get a call from a stockbroker touting some deal, an undervalued stock, and that if you buy today you're sure to make a lot of money, the odds are great that you will not buy today, or ever, from that person. But if you get a call from your personal stockbroker offering *the exact same* stock, using the exact same language as the stranger did, it is more likely that you will buy the stock because of the fact that you trust the person on the other end of the phone.

NOTE WELL: Because trust is so subjective, because trust is so volatile, because trust is so fickle, and because trust is so judgmental, I've tried to define as many aspects of trust as I can, in order for you to see the nuance of the trust process. Because it's the highest level of human and social interaction, it's also the most complex.

But the simplicity of trust is if you don't have it from others, it's because you have not earned it. If you don't give trust to others, it's because they haven't earned it.

The big secret to earning trust is to uncover why it doesn't exist at this moment and work bit by bit to gain it. The bigger secret is that once you have trust, you must fight to keep trust. But the biggest secret is in order to get trust, you have to be trustworthy and give trust.

"Of course I trust you. You have an honest face. In fact, you remind me of myself!"

The 14.5 definitions of trust

Trust is everywhere – it's ubiquitous and omnipotent

1. The risk of trust and trusting – trust is a risk.

2. Initial trust is tentative.

3. Trust is a form of faith.

4. Trust lowers resistance.

5. Trust lowers barriers.

6. Friendship leads to trust.

7. Business relationships lead to trust.

8. Business deals are based on trust.

9. Dealings over time lead to trust.

10. Sales are based on trust.

11. Trust is the link between yes and no.

12. Trust is a green light.

13. Personal relationships lead to trust.

14. Marriage is based on love and trust.

14.5 Trust breeds confidence – in yourself and from others.

23.5 characteristics of trusted and trustworthy people

"Few delights can equal the presence of one whom we trust utterly."

– George MacDonald

23.5 characteristics of trusted and trustworthy people

Stories clarify thoughts and statements. If you look at *Aesop's Fables*, he tells a story and makes a point or teaches a moral. It's no different in teaching trust, understanding trust, or being trustworthy.

Below are characteristics of trust from human to human, and the stories that will clarify those characteristics.

As with all stories, they may make you think of your own. I hope they do, because that will clarify the characteristics of trust for you.

When I first moved to Charlotte in 1988, I had no money. I had a consulting contract and a challenge to build someone else's business magazine by interviewing top business people and selling ads. My very first sales call was to Jim Riggins at his copier and office equipment company called Technocom.

From a telephone cold call, to a face-to-face appointment, to an hour and a half of explanation and dialogue, Jim bought a full-page color ad, and gave me a check on the spot. He then asked what I was doing for a copier. Sheepishly, I said, "It's not in the budget right now, but the minute it is, you'll have my business," and left.

The following morning, there was a knock on my apartment/office door. It was a delivery guy with a copier. "Jim Riggins said to deliver this to you and told me to tell you that you can use it for free until you can afford to pay for it." I was stunned.

That was 20 years and about $250,000 worth of business ago. Riggins continues to be a trusted personal friend.

Over the years, Jim Riggins and I have exchanged intimate, confidential business advice. I've done several commercials for his company and have provided training sessions, at no charge. And based on that initial surprise delivery that day, I still feel like I owe him.

There are many trust characteristics to this story – not the least of which is **to get trust, first give trust**. Another one is **surprise (genuine) help leads to trust**. Another one is **trust grows slowly over time**.

Flying on my way to I can't remember where, the guy in the aisle next to me looked like someone I would like to meet, so we began to talk.

His name was Walter Putnam. He's an insurance agent for Northwestern Mutual Life. "Oh," I said, "I just did a seminar for your healthcare division. I'll bet you're friends with Suzy Johnson." "I am," he said. "I work with her all the time."

Walter asked me if I had ever addressed the Million Dollar Round Table. I said no. He asked if I would like to. I said sure. He told me that he was on the selection committee and that he would see what he could do.

Three interviews in front of the selection committee, some editing of my content for language, and 120 days later, there I was on the main platform, addressing some 5,000 insurance agents from all over the world, because of serendipity, networking, and Walter Putnam.

Giving value first leads to trust.

Fast forward two years… I had no "financial plan," realized that it was about time to make one for my family, and further realized that my new friend Walter Putnam would probably be my planner of choice.

Though Walter and I had several personal meetings over the past two years, none would be considered a sales call. Lunch. A ball game. A fundraiser. Social. One day he came to my home with his briefcase for a formalized sales call.

His first question was, "Who are your three most trusted advisors?" Stunned at how challenging and unique the question was, I began by saying, "Walter, that might be the best question I've ever been asked." (Note well that I'm a student and an expert at the science of asking questions that differentiate me from my competitors. I've written tens of thousands of words on the topic. And Walter's question just topped my list.)

I had to stop and think. After a short space of time, I gave him three names. "Tell me a little bit about each one," he said. So I did. And then Walter went emotionally to what I've referred to as the second level of questioning. He said, "Jeffrey, tell me about how each one became a trusted advisor for you." At the end of the first story, I was crying.

By the end of the third story, I was mentally writing him a check. He had won my trust both logically and emotionally. And I have been writing him checks every month for the past 10 years.

Questions that differentiate, especially in matters of money, lead to trust.

I live in an old factory in Charlotte, North Carolina. It's a wooden building with a brick façade that was built in the 1930s.

I began buying units and opening walls to connect them. I needed a contractor. I called my friend Katie Tyler and asked her for a recommendation. "Mike Allen of Twelve Stone Construction," she said without a moment of hesitation. "He'll be perfect for you."

The first project I gave Mike was a simple one – cut a hole in the wall between two of my units and mount two antique doors into the hole. His work was superior, but his on-the-job cleanliness was remarkable. He actually left the job site cleaner than it was when he started. And I'm not just saying at the end of the job – I'm saying at the end of each day that he worked on the job.

I've watched construction since the time I was a child. My father built homes and had a kitchen cabinet manufacturing company. I have NEVER seen anything or known any contractor like Mike Allen.

Since the first job I gave him 10 years ago, there have been 100 others. The jobs have ranged from a 14-foot spiral staircase to patchwork on drywall. During that 10-year period of time, I developed trust in Mike Allen and also got to know him as a person. Part of his life is missionary work. He's a family man. He's a student. (He reads my books.) And we're friends. His competency, his superior skill, and (yes) his remarkable cleanliness have led me to trust him.

Competency and superior skill leads to trust.

I needed a succession plan. I have a little bit of money now, and I wanted to make sure that the details of things like a will, a trust for some of my collectibles, and my last wishes for who would inherit what, be committed to writing in the least government-intrusive way.

I have several long-time attorney friends in Charlotte who specialize in this type of thing. I called and made a few appointments and told each friend that I was looking to select only one. My 20-year legal and personal friend Rick Marsh showed up.

By way of credentials, Rick Marsh is an attorney with a Masters in tax. He's also a CPA, and he's an MBA. Not too shabby. He walks in. We greet each other all smiles. He has a thick file folder.

And before I can say anything beyond pleasantries, he pulls out a 5x7 picture of a government building in a small gold frame and sets it up on the table.

"Do you know what this building is?" he inquired. "Not really," I said. "Looks like some government building."

Marsh replied, "This is a picture of the Internal Revenue Service. I'm giving it to you as a gift. I want you to put it on your desk where you will see it every day, and think about this... At the end of your life, one of two things is going to happen. Either the government will get your money, or your children will get your money. And I'm here today to make certain that your money goes to your kids."

"You're hired!" I said.

Without a doubt, Rick's presentation was the most creative and compelling one-minute sales presentation I have ever witnessed. Yes, I still have the picture on my desk. And after two months of data and detail back and forth, all the documents are done and signed. I feel like the weight of the world is off my shoulders. And I feel like I selected a person with a passion for making certain that I will be protected. I unequivocally trust Rick Marsh.

Straight-forward truth leads to trust, creativity leads to trust, and WOW! leads to trust.

I went to a power breakfast in Charlotte, North Carolina to hear Arthur Blank, cofounder of Home Depot, deliver a keynote address to Charlotte's most prominent business people. At the end of his talk, he collected a fat check for his speaking fee and then went to play golf with Arnold Palmer. His tee time was so close to the completion of his talk that he showed up wearing a golf shirt.

Sitting at my table of 10 were two people that I kind of knew: a banker who had switched from my bank at the time (First Citizens) to The Scottish Bank, and a young entrepreneur named Brian Parsley. Brian had just sold his business, an Internet recruiting and job placement company, and was searching for what to do next.

Two things happened that day. The banker offered me a loan to get our relationship going. (I took it and still have that line of credit. That was in 1999.) And Brian and I talked. He indicated he might like to try his hand at professional speaking. "Come on over," I said. "Hang out at my office for a while and see how you like it." He did, and he's been hanging around ever since. First he became a business manager. Then I gave him a few speaking assignments where I was double-booked and allowed him to use my material. Brian was an instant hit. Audiences loved him.

I filmed him, coached him, filmed him again, coached him again, attended a dozen of his speeches, coached him 12 more times, and today (some 8 years later) I'm still coaching him – as a mentor and as a friend. Brian is eager to accept my coaching and he's responsive to my advice. And each time he speaks, he gets better.

Brian has achieved speaking excellence in an exceptionally short space of time, based on his personal dedication, his openness to learn, and his intelligence to transfer that wisdom to an audience.

I trust Brian Parsley to deliver my message, with his nuance, to my customers. He has proven himself several hundred times in all kinds of circumstances. I understand and respect what he goes through as a speaker and I hope to spend the next 20 years watching him grow and blossom.

Giving trust leads to getting trust.

Early in my business career, I sought counsel from my father. I wanted his advice because I trusted it, and I respected it. It seemed to bond us. Even though he was somewhat cynical and negative, it did not affect his intelligence or the correctness of his advice.

"Lawyers are for legal advice, not for business advice," he would often say. I held that piece of advice as sacrosanct until I met Mickey Aberman, a likeable attorney who looks more professorial than legal and whose insight carries way beyond the law.

Not just a brilliant attorney, Mickey Aberman is a brilliant person. He's able to look at a contract and tell me what the ramifications are five years down the road. He looks at intent, content, legality, impact, ramifications, consequences, and the spirit of everything I put in front of him. And he does it with amazing speed.

He has broken my barrier of taking business advice from an attorney. And that barrier will stay broken for as long as our relationship exists.

Over the past decade, Mickey Aberman has also become my friend. There's an occasional breakfast or lunch and always an annual invitation extended to him to attend my company's Christmas party (even though we're both Jewish).

Superior knowledge and genuine help lead to trust.

I got a call one Saturday morning from my banker at First Citizens, William Braddy. We met at Einstein's Bagels, where he told me that the bank would no longer support me or my business and that the same was true for several other entrepreneurs who were his customers. As a result, he was leaving the bank.

YIKES! Braddy had been my banker and my friend for 6 years, and First Citizens had been my bank for 17 years.

Now what?

William told me that he'd set up a meeting for me with a friend of his at Wachovia Bank, and he assured me they would welcome my business. After several weeks of frustration trying to connect with a person whose title was "Wealth Banker," I became frustrated at his lack of timely response. Evidently I was not that wealthy.

I sent an email to the people this guy was dealing with inside the bank, explaining my frustration. Within one hour, a woman named Cameron Williams (now Cameron Uher) called me on the phone to reassure me that indeed the bank wanted my business, that indeed she was in charge, and that indeed things would begin to happen rapidly. She was correct.

After a series of interviews, and normal bank scrutiny, I was given an unsecured bridge loan, a line of credit, and a new mortgage to replace an existing loan at another bank where a large balloon payment was coming due, literally within the week.

In short, Cameron Uher rescued the financial well-being of my business. Since that time, she has been one of the most responsive, helpful, proactive people in the banking world that I have had the pleasure of dealing with. I trust her at her word, and I respect her for her capability and genuine desire to serve.

Superior service leads to trust, understanding leads to trust, and willingness to help leads to trust.

NOTE TO ENTREPRENEURS: For those of you who have faced or are facing a similar situation to what I encountered, I want you to know why I switched a 17-year banking relationship in 24 hours. Wachovia Bank and the people they assigned to my account, including Cameron, understood my business and were willing to do something about it. There are many banks that claim, in their politically correct advertising, "We understand your business," but very few, when it comes down to taking action, are willing to step up to the plate. Wachovia Bank was willing. If you're an entrepreneur, perhaps you might give Cameron a call.

I drive a Lexus. I could drive any car, but I choose Lexus because of their service and reliability. Not just any Lexus – a Lexus from Hendrick Lexus of Charlotte.

At Hendrick Lexus, Brian Gendron is the manager, Chris Calder is the service manager, and my two sales guys are Gant Howell and Butch Hammett.

Sounds like I'm a big customer. But really I'm not. I've only purchased two cars for myself in the past ten years. Because of traveling and speaking, I only drive about 2,000 miles a year. (I fill my tank once a month.)

I bought my first Hendrick Lexus sedan in 1998, and when I gave it to my daughter Rebecca nine years later, it had only 24,000 miles on it.

In 2007, I bought a new red Lexus. A year later, I thought to myself that maybe I'd trade it in for another new one because it only had 2,000 miles on it. I called Butch and told him what I wanted to do and went down to meet him, figuring that for a few thousand dollars I could upgrade my car. Butch informed me that the cost to flip would be around $9,000 and he advised me that the body styles would be exactly the same, and to wait a couple years for a time when the deal would make more sense.

Keep in mind that Butch Hammett, as nice a guy as he is, is a car salesman. He only gets paid when a car is sold. But it turns out he's a car salesman with a conscience.

I was elated that he was so honest with me and left without a new car. Ninety days later, my daughter Stacey, who lives in Palm Beach County, Florida, had an automobile lease that was about to expire. She was looking for a Lexus. So I called the Lexus dealership in Boca Raton and asked to speak to the sales manager.

A guy came on the phone, and the first thing he told me was that they're the largest Lexus dealership in the country and that they could get me a great deal at the lowest prices in the country on any Lexus I wanted, blah, blah, yadda, yadda. I said, "Great. I'd like a white IS250 with grey leather and GPS."

Two days later he calls me back to again remind me they were the largest Lexus dealer in the U.S. He tells me that they don't have an IS250 in white with grey leather, and he can't find one with GPS anywhere in the Southeast. He asks me if I would be willing to take another color because they could deliver something else (that I didn't want) right away. He seemed to be in a hurry. I asked him to keep looking for a white one. He agreed, said he would call me back, and hung up. He never called me back.

Four days later, I called (honest) Butch at Hendrick Lexus in Charlotte. "Butch, can you sell a car to someone who lives in Florida?" "Sure," he said. "Can you arrange for Florida tags and taxes?" "Sure," he said. "Do you happen to have a white IS250 in stock with grey leather and GPS?" "Let me check," he said.

He comes back to the phone in under a minute and says, "Got it! I can sell it to you for $XXXXX," (which was several hundred dollars LESS than Boca Lexus – the largest Lexus dealer in the U.S.), and I said, "I'll take it."

Stacey picked up the car, drove it from Charlotte to Florida without a hitch and is now having the car locally serviced at any dealership BUT Boca Lexus.

Back to Butch Hammett. Butch's honesty and integrity kept him top of mind, and combined with my past experience at Hendrick Lexus, created that selling (buying) opportunity.

The interesting characteristic about this story of trust is that I trust Lexus, I trust the car itself (it's been my friend for 10 years and never failed me), and I trust Butch and all the people at Hendrick Lexus. If you've ever had a lousy experience at a car dealership and believe in your mind that all car dealerships are pretty much the same, call Hendrick Lexus; you'll get a different perspective.

Truth and honest dealings lead to trust.

Bob Carr is an entrepreneur. His company, TLC in Baltimore, installs sprinkler systems and exterior lighting. Recently he has expanded his business to install Christmas lighting and organize people's messy garages and basements using a slat wall technique, hanging everything that used to be on the floor. The before and after pictures are amazing.

Bob is a six-year client and friend of mine. Bob is also a student of success.

He dedicates about 30 days a year to his own growth by attending seminars and workshops all around the country. It's working. Bob is successful. I respect him.

Three years ago I helped him create an email magazine that now has thousands of subscribers. Like mine, his email magazine comes out every Tuesday morning. He's never missed an issue. That track record paints a very small picture of Bob's greatest asset: *reliability*.

Bob has 30 work crews out on the road at any given time and makes all kinds of promises to his customers regarding installations and maintenance. Bob keeps his promises. In the rare instance that something goes wrong, Bob takes personal responsibility and will often visit a customer to face (and handle) the situation one on one.

Story after story has emerged about Bob Carr going the extra mile and spending the extra dollar for his customers. I helped create two testimonial DVDs for Bob, letting his customers tell the TLC story. His dedication to excellence has earned the respect and loyalty of his customers – me included.

Bob has also installed slat walls in one of my lofts. Paul and Chris, his carpenters, performed flawlessly on three different occasions. I've called on Bob not less than 50 times to ask for something, and 50 times Bob has delivered faster and better than I expected. Bob is also always in a great mood, and has a great attitude. (Attitude is one of the things that Bob studies.) Bob Carr is reliable, is respected, has a great work ethic, has a great attitude, and is making money. I wonder if those attributes have something in common.

Respect and reliability over time leads to trust.

"Hi, this is Mark McDonald. I love to serve…" That's the opening line of Mark McDonald's voicemail and an insight into his character.

Mark is the Sales Cowboy at my online training company, TrainOne. He often accompanies me to seminars and always arrives in the morning an hour before I do to meet the customer and get ready for the event. He handles everything from setting up books in the back of the room, to making sure a double espresso with a splash of coffee greets me upon arrival, to selling multi-million dollar training contracts – all with a smile on his face.

In our staff meetings when I go around the room and ask each person to say a few words about what's going on, Mark always begins by saying how grateful he is to work at the company, be with me, and work with all the great people that we have in our family.

Mark is also a successful, elephant-hunting salesperson. He is able to successfully connect with Fortune 500 company decision makers at every level and make the sale. He can talk to the CEO, the head of training, a committee of decision makers, or a delivery guy in the warehouse, with intelligence and respect.

His humility and willingness to serve earns him the loyalty and trust that he deserves, without ever having to ask for it. People are truthful with Mark because they know he is truthful with them.

Personally I have often remarked that Mark McDonald is one of nicest people, if not *the* nicest person, I've ever met.

Desire to serve with a grateful heart leads to trust.

I met Don Green three years ago at the National Speakers Association annual meeting. We were introduced by Charlie "Tremendous" Jones. Don is the executive director of the Napoleon Hill Foundation.

I'm a student and dedicated follower of Napoleon Hill. Having read almost all of his writings, I attribute my achievement of a positive attitude in large part to reading *Think & Grow Rich* 10 times in 1972. (Sounds nutty, but it worked.)

I invited Don to Charlotte to see my business and my collection of Napoleon Hill books and ephemera. As a result of our mutual love of Napoleon Hill and personal development in general, we became fast friends.

I offered to create the Napoleon Hill email magazine to make more of Hill's philosophies and writings known to the thousands of people who visit his website each day, and I offered to do it at no charge.

I felt it was the least that I could do based on what Napoleon Hill had done for me. As I write this passage, we just passed weekly issue number 76 (which by coincidence came out on the 4th of July). I'll be doing several other projects with the Napoleon Hill Foundation – some of which might even involve financial remuneration.

The main reason that I'm willing to do them is my faith and trust in Don Green as a person.

Don is wealthy and retired. He doesn't need the Napoleon Hill Foundation; rather he is *dedicated* to the Napoleon Hill Foundation. And it's that dedication that has inspired me to become involved.

Dedication to serving and enlightening others based on heartfelt belief leads to trust.

I met Richard Greaves in 1981 in Milwaukee. He was a factory worker at a screen printing plant. Along with my consulting partner, Duke Daulton, we recommended that Richard be made plant manager.

The client took the recommendation, and we coached Richard on the success characteristics of running a factory.

He was a willing, grateful, and exceptionally responsive student who rose above the task.

Richard became frustrated with his employer, and I found him another job running a screen printing factory in California.

Then, in 1983, I decided to open up another garment
manufacturing and printing company and immediately
called Richard to run the plant. Everything had to be
set up from scratch – machines, art department, screen
burning, and every aspect of textile screen printing.
Working 18 hours a day, living in an apartment three
blocks away from the factory, running home every day to
record an episode of *Monty Python's Flying Circus*, Richard
set up a phenomenal and smooth-running operation.

I was flying around the country making sales while Richard
was dutifully in the factory drinking Mountain Dew, working
double shifts, and exceeding production expectations.

One day on the road, I become deathly ill with the flu
and had to fly back home to Philadelphia at a moment's
notice. The night before, there was a major snowstorm that
dumped more than two feet of snow all over the city. My
car was in the airport parking lot, buried.

I had no idea what to expect when my plane landed. All
I could think about was somehow getting my car out of
wherever it was stuck and getting home to a nice, warm
bed where I could vegetate and recover. Stumbling
through baggage claim, sick as a dog, and boarding a bus
to long-term parking, I dreaded finding my car buried
under two feet of snow.

Not surprisingly, I forgot exactly where I had parked my
car and made the bus driver go on a tour of the parking
lot to where I thought it might be. "Here it is!" I screamed.
The parking lot was a blanket of snow. Every car was
buried except for one.

One car was completely clean and dug out all the way to the aisle, providing a clear path to exit. Immediately, I knew who did it. Richard Greaves had driven 30 miles from the factory, somehow found my car in the parking lot, and completely removed every flake of snow from the car and the surrounding area.

That was 25 years ago, and I still thank Richard every time I see him.

Random acts of kindness and the desire to do the best job possible lead to trust.

Jessica McDougall is my partner, my best friend, and the creative director for all my book projects (like this one). In her role as my "secret weapon," she accompanies me to all my speaking events and helps me get ready to present. She is amazing as a worker and as a person. We spend 24-7 together in harmony, for months at a time.

Early on in our relationship, we had a discussion about what to do in a particular situation. She wanted it one way; I wanted it the other. I got a bit hot under the collar at her insistence on doing it her way, since I KNEW my way was better. After about 30 minutes of not speaking, she came up to me and spoke softly. "I have your best interest at heart." Weak in the knees, I thanked her and have since always given her the benefit of the doubt.

Jessica has proven herself to be correct for the past three years. Her genuine interest, her dedication to excellence, and her heart have won my trust, and much more.

Accurate advice over time and friendship without condition or expectation lead to trust.

I hired Michelle (Gerard) Joyce right after her college graduation in the summer of 1997.

Her job was receiving and sending faxes from my weekly column that appeared in papers all over the country. We were getting hundreds of faxes each day. She was eager. She was smart. She had a great attitude. I began giving her more and more responsibilities such as answering the phones and getting more involved in the business.

One afternoon she had an altercation with my public relations person. It seems the PR woman had a need to put others down rather than help them. She came to me and said, "I can't get along with Michelle. One of us has to go." So I fired her and kept Michelle.

Two months later, the woman booking my seminars got pregnant and moved back to St. Louis. I put Michelle in her position. That was 10 years ago.

Over a 10-year period of time, Michelle Joyce has blossomed into the best speaker and seminar booker in the United States. Not only does she book over 200 events a year, she also gives seminars and consults others based on her expertise. In short, she has gained my trust by performing in a superior manner, with superior ability, year after year.

I also believe that Michelle has set a world record for crying in my office. Her passion for excellence and her desire to improve are both key components in her achievement process. And, like anyone with passion, she's emotional about it. She is always seeking to do the best job in the best way, and the vast majority of the time she does.

I don't consider Michelle an employee of my company. Rather, I consider her a daughter in my family.

Superior performance with passion over time leads to trust.

My brother Josh is a spiritual and gentle soul of the earth. His friendly, engaging, and reserved manner generate instant likeability in all who meet him and know him.

Among other attributes (choir leader, gardener, ping pong player, and calligrapher), Josh is a world-class graphic designer. For more than 30 years, he designed everything by hand, refusing to enter the computer age.

Four years ago, I bought him a computer. Reluctantly he began to use it and found it was better and faster than the old-fashioned way.

Josh has since become a world-class expert at computer graphic design. He has evolved into a full-time employee, and become an integral person at Buy Gitomer and TrainOne. Every day, some new design or graphic appears with Josh's trademark of excellence stamped all over it.

Book covers, promotional pieces, graphics for public seminars, CD products, and the Buy Gitomer website have all been completed in a way that displays a continuation of my brand and an excellence that can only be marveled at each time something new appears. From the trash can and the magic sales answer ball to *The Sales Bible* cover redesign and each page of the Gitomer website, Josh's superior talent and taste have earned him the respect and trust of every person on the Buy Gitomer and TrainOne teams, and I'll put myself at the top of that list.

On the writing retreat for the completion of this book, I asked that one of each of my products be shipped there for reference and inspiration. Each one of them has my brother Josh stamped all over them. It's not just a sight to behold. It's a sight to be proud of and grateful for.

Dedication to personal excellence and mastery of a craft leads to trust.

There are all sorts of levels of trust. Obviously trust has to be proven over some period of time, but once achieved, trusted advice from people at the top of their profession can be both reassuring and comforting.

Everyone needs the advice of trusted experts, but in my experience their trusted expertise is delivered with far greater impact when a friendship has also been established.

In addition to those people mentioned in the previous stories, another of my best friends is Bob Salvin, entrepreneur of the first order.

Bob called me one morning to congratulate me on my front-page article in the *Charlotte Observer*. He was genuinely proud of me. He knew I was on a writing retreat, and he wanted to FedEx me a copy of the article and a bag of pistachio nuts. "How can you be your creative best without a bag of pistachio nuts?" he asked.

He's not just a great friend; he's a great guy.

Other trusted friends include – Nikita Koloff, retired professional wrestler turned minister and missionary; Mitchell Kearney, photographer, or should I say "artist" with a camera; and Richard Brodie, creator of Microsoft Word 1.0, thinker, world traveler, and professional poker player.

There's also Ray Leone, sales trainer of the first order; Jersey Boy of the first order. Ed Brodow, expert on negotiation, gave one of the best seminars on "how to present" I have ever seen.

Victoria Labalme, a genuine NYC crazy-busy woman, studied under Marcel Marceau, and is a captivating presenter/performer. Giovanni Livera, one of the world's greatest close-up magicians, master of his craft and creative off the charts; his performances are electric.

In the speaking business three people stand alone as heroes – Ty Boyd, my other dad who got me involved and encouraged me all the way. Nido Qubein, the essence of class, who taught me that the right way is the best way.

And Charlie "Tremendous" Jones, who is the single best example of how to speak, how to live, and how to die.

On the writing side, my hat goes off to Harvey Mackay, the consummate writer and book promoter, whose off-handed advice in our casual conversations has served me well.

Doc Hersey, creator of *Situational Leadership* and author of many books, has set a standard for how to write and grow an educational company. The Center for Leadership Studies stands alone as the standard of excellence.

And the writing list would not be complete without Ray Bard, whose idea and inspiration for *The Little Red Book of Selling* helped launch my brand as an author.

Sometimes (if you're lucky) your customers become friends. Jim Feltman is one of them. Chief Marketing Officer is his title, but great person, devoted husband, father and grandfather, thinker, student, and a man who takes action for the good of all is a better description.

And this list must also include Earl Pertnoy, a person of wealth, a man of honor, a brilliant thinker, and a friend and mentor for more than 30 years. We talk, we laugh, I listen, I learn, I trust, and I am grateful.

I have given you but a few examples of people who inspire me, encourage me, help me without expectation, and are my friends.

I love them. And I trust them in times of happiness and in times of need.

Friendship based on respect, mutual admiration, truth, and fun leads to trust.

Here are some questions to ask yourself as you seek to discover who your trusted friends are?

Who are your BEST friends?

What are the elements of those friendships?

How were they built?

Who is your single BEST friend?

Is it someone who understands you?

Is it someone who is there for you?

Is it someone you trust?

There's one final characteristic. It's the glue that binds all the other characteristics together and it's the fuel that allows me to trust others:

I trust myself first.

As a writer, a speaker, an entrepreneur, an idea person, a friend, and especially as a dad and a grandfather, I believe in my heart that I'm the most trustworthy person I know, and I respect the trust I get from, and have in, others.

23.5 characteristics of trusted and trustworthy People

From my personal life experiences, here are the 23.5 characteristics that I have discovered in other people that have led me to trust them:

1. To get trust, first give trust.

2. Surprise (genuine) help leads to trust.

3. Trust grows slowly over time.

4. Giving value first leads to trust.

5. Questions that differentiate, especially in matters of money, lead to trust.

6. Competency and superior skill leads to trust.

7. Straight-forward truth leads to trust.

8. Creativity leads to trust.

9. WOW! leads to trust.

10. Giving trust leads to getting trust.

11. Superior knowledge and genuine help lead to trust.

12. Superior service leads to trust.

13. Understanding leads to trust.

14. Willingness to help leads to trust.

15. Truth and honest dealings lead to trust.

16. Respect and reliability over time leads to trust.

17. Desire to serve with a grateful heart leads to trust.

18. Dedication to serving and enlightening others based on heartfelt belief leads to trust.

19. Random acts of kindness and the desire to do the best job possible lead to trust.

20. Accurate advice over time and friendship without condition or expectation lead to trust.

21. Superior performance with passion over time leads to trust.

22. Dedication to personal excellence and mastery of a craft leads to trust.

23. Friendship based on respect, mutual admiration, truth, and fun leads to trust.

23.5 I trust myself first.

Business and sales advice you can trust... and bank on

"You may be deceived if you trust too much, but you will live in torment if you do not trust enough."

– Frank Crane

I found someone I trust.

I just got off the phone with Mike Levine. He's expanding his business and needs a general manager. His opening sentence to me was "I found someone I trust." He didn't say, "I found the most competent person on the planet." He didn't say, "I found someone with incredible experience." He didn't say, "I found the most organized person in the world." He didn't say, "I found the perfect person for my position of general manager."

No. He said, "I found someone I *trust*."

Trust was his highest criterion for making the hire, and it was the first thing he spoke about when telling me his story. Obviously it was his highest priority.

There were thousands, maybe millions, of people who were qualified to be his general manager but only a handful or less that he could put in the category of trusted.

I wonder how many people, when filling out their résumé for a job or a career change, use the word "trust" or "trustworthy" when describing themselves. Let me give you the answer to that: few or none.

Are you the real (sales) thing? Chances are you're not!

The authentic salesperson. Is that you?

You probably think you are, and you're probably wrong. So wrong, in fact, that by the time you're finished reading this, the pain will be so intense, you may actually take some action to make yourself more authentic.

> Everyone seeks to be known as authentic. Very few are.

If I asked you how authentic you are, your answer would be "10!" on the one-to-ten scale. But if I asked you how authentic your customers perceive you to be, would your answer be the same? Or maybe a little lower? Or maybe a lot lower?

What is authentic? It's something EVERY salesperson strives to be. The real question is HOW AUTHENTIC ARE YOU? To find out, rate how close to "10" you are on the authenticity scale in each of these 10.5 categories?

1. Long-term relationships with customers – What percentage of your customers have been with you for more than five years? They are the measure of your authenticity, and will often tell others about it.

2. Excellent market exposure and position – Are you positioned in a way that others in your industry (especially your customers and prospects) see you, and see the value in what you do, what you represent, and how you help others?

3. Great reputation in your industry – What do people in your industry say about you behind your back? How are you regarded?

4. High respect of customers, coworkers, and community – How does your close-in network regard you? What is your reputation among them?

5. Friendly, likeable, and sincere in helping others – The more you help others, the more your authenticity grows. No limits.

6. Reliable as a person – Do what you say you will do. Be there when you say you will be there. Be someone that others can count on. Be there when you are needed.

7. Reliable as a resource – Have knowledge. Have wisdom. Have answers. Have connections and an informal network of influential people. Be in the know, and be willing to share it.

8. Perceived value provider – Who benefits from your actions? Only you? Do you write? Anyone save what you write? Do people send in and ask for a copy?

9. Personally branded – What is your reputation? Who knows you? What are others saying about you? What do people think when they see your name? What do you want them to think?

10. Published and perceived as an authority – Got articles? Got book? If not, you're missing a big piece (maybe THE piece) of authenticity.

10.5 You get unsolicited referrals on a regular basis – The authentic salesperson gets a report card every day. Not your paycheck, not your referrals – it's your UNSOLICITED referrals.

High score is 110. How'd you do?

The more authentic you are *perceived* to be, the more likely the customer or the prospect or the probable purchaser will buy from you.

THERE'S A BONUS: Your authenticity, if it's high, will also give you a competitive advantage that may preclude price as an issue.

The world's greatest heart surgeon does not have to justify price. He's authentic. Everyone knows it. And everyone pays his asking price.

You see, when I ask if you are an authentic salesperson, I'm not asking that question in terms of how you perceive yourself. That's not what authenticity is. Authenticity, or the authentic salesperson, comes from how your customers, your marketplace, and even your coworkers *perceive* you.

There's an old sales adage that goes: In sales, it's not who you know; in sales, it's who knows you. Authentic salespeople are well known.

If you're well known by your coworkers, that doesn't count. If you're well known by your customers, that almost counts. If you're well known by your prospective customers, that counts. If you're well known in your industry, that really counts.

THE BIG QUESTION IS: How do you become well known? Because the more known you are, the more authentic you are perceived to be.

YOU'RE IN LUCK: There are steps you can take to become better known and be perceived as more authentic.

NOTE WELL: Part of being authentic is being honorable and being real. Regardless of what you do to gain notoriety, if you're below an ethical standard, or people perceive you as being insincere, your authenticity will only be perceived as low level. Yes, you will be well known, but the question is: For what and as what?

The best way to test your present authenticity is to go to Google.com, enter your name, and hit return. What happened? Nothing? Not much? A few things? I use Google as a measuring stick for notoriety and authenticity. So do your customers. So do your prospects. So do your industry leaders. They Google you, just like you Google them. So your first job is to understand that by being Google-able, you are on the path to some degree of authenticity. Google is an authenticity report card. What grade did you get?

There are 7.5 actions that you can take within the next 30 days that will get you on Internet search engines and help you gain some immediate authenticity:

1. Get a website that has your name.com. If your name is taken, figure out a website name that includes your name, like www.thegreatjeffrey.com. By establishing and building your own website, you will immediately be listed on every search engine on the planet. Then, what you do with your website will begin to build your authenticity. The content of your website must be of interest and of help to your customers. It must contain ideas, tips, best practices, articles, and information that helps your customers win. Helping others leads to authenticity.

2. Write a white paper. Your ability to write about your industry, how your customers use your product to produce and profit, or success stories of others, will establish you as a thinker. Writing your definitive philosophies will separate you from others. Writing is hard, perhaps the hardest task of a salesperson, but not only does it contribute to your authenticity, it also makes selling easier. Does your prospect want your third-rate business card and self-indulgent brochure? Or do they want the white paper you just wrote on how they can produce more and profit more? Obviously that's a rhetorical question, but it can't be that obvious because you're not doing it.

3. An article that your customers, prospects, or other people in your industry will read. Shorter than a white paper, an article focuses on a single subject that may have to do with issues of service, morale, a productive idea, a strategy, a philosophy, or even a success story.

Your article should be strategically placed in a trade journal, newsletter, or local business paper and ALSO emailed to every person on your list. If you don't have a list, what are you thinking?

4. Your weekly communication to your entire base of contacts. Mine is an email magazine called *Sales Caffeine*. It's a free subscription that contains helpful sales information and ideas that others can use and profit from. It's also viral. There's enough good information in it to where one sales person is compelled to forward it to another salesperson. This increases and expands my authenticity (and your authenticity should you choose to use this medium).

NOTE WELL: The single most valuable asset you will possess over the next 50 years will be your email mailing list. Build it, use it to help others profit, and guard it with your life.

5. Speak at a conference. Don't just be an attendee or an exhibitor. Speaking to your peers assures you a leadership position and an authenticity that is undeniable. Speaking means that you are an expert or an authority, that you have prepared, and that your presentation skills are competent enough to face a group of peers and win their hearts and minds.

6. Become a leader of something. By taking a leadership role in a community event, a business group, or on a committee, you are showing others a willingness to accept responsibility and complete a task to the best of your ability. That authenticity goes a long way toward creating the next critical component: reputation.

7. Build a great reputation. If you add up all of your deeds, all of your good will, all of your word-of-mouth rumblings, and all of your achievements, together they equal your reputation. If you complain to me that you don't have much of a reputation, it's because you haven't taken many actions to create one. If you complain to me that your reputation is great but that your company's reputation leaves something to be desired, then get out of there. Your company's reputation and your reputation must be in total harmony, and be totally congruent, in order for you to have true authenticity.

7.5 Fake it till you make it… ALMOST. In order to be authentic, you have to live authentically. The problem is you can't start out authentic; you have to be a student of authenticity. You have to take daily actions that will lead you to a greater degree of authenticity. During that period of time, you have to act authentic. I'm not saying be insincere. I'm saying *live the part.* I'm not saying be someone you're not; I'm saying *be who you want to become.* You grow into authenticity by taking authentic actions, and there's nothing wrong with the self-belief process of knowing where you're going and living it until you get there. I could have just as easily named this point "live the part," but I think it's important to understand that you will start out being someone that you are not, or better said, not yet. Authenticity builds… as you build it.

HERE'S A GREAT WAY TO BUILD A FOUNDATION: *Help others because it makes you feel good.* The more help you share, the more help is returned to you – not by the individual, but by everyone.

What makes you authentic? The consistent positive actions you take that build your personal brand and your reputation.

NOTE WELL: Authenticity is never a part of someone's "system of selling" – that's why I'm against all systems. Systems focus on the "selling" process. Mistake. Big mistake. Authentic people create buying atmospheres with all the OTHER things they do that get them to the sales meeting.

Is that you? It better be, or you will lose to someone who is.

> The authenticity of the sale is in the salesperson. If you're authentic, you don't have to say it or prove it. It shows and speaks for itself. The most powerful part of authenticity is that, if done properly, it's unspoken.

PERSONAL NOTE: When I go into a sales call, my authenticity is not my business card. My authenticity is my book. Autographed. Which sales educator or sales trainer do you think gets the job – the one who read the book, or the one who wrote the book?

Will the REAL presenter please stand up?

There's an old expression that goes, "Sincerity is the key. If you can fake that, you've got it made." As a presenter, you have a responsibility to deliver a believable, passionate, meaningful, authentic message that the audience can relate to and learn from.

Knowing these fundamental and easy-to-understand facts, you'd think that all speakers would get it and deliver it. And you would be wrong.

As in sales, the audience must first buy the speaker before they buy the speaker's message.

The key is *perceived* authenticity. Presenting a real-world, relatable, and transferable message. That's a presenter's responsibility and an audience member's hope.

And let me bust one bubble. If you're thinking to yourself, "I'm authentic," it doesn't matter what you think. It only matters what the audience thinks, and you've probably never put yourself to the authenticity test.

Well, I'm about to.

On the next four pages are the elements of authenticity. Rather than just reading them, why not rate yourself from 1 – 10 in the process? You may "know" the elements of authenticity, but you may not be the master of them.

Authentic is:

- **Being prepared in terms of the audience.** Not just with "your talk" or "your story."

- **Being honest with the audience and yourself.** Sometimes presenters tell a lie so often that they begin to believe it's the truth.

- **Being truthful about your stories and your facts.** The big fish that got away seems to get bigger as years go by.

- **Offering information that's useable.** You may not know what useable information is either, but the audience knows it the second they hear it. That's why people take notes.

- **Being relaxed in style and demeanor.** Presenting from a position of comfort is actually more powerful than trying to be authoritative. When you relax, the audience relaxes, and your message is openly received.

- **Being personal and engaging in your message and your presentation manner.** You need to be real without being maudlin or compromising. Have information that directly affects the audience, and speak candidly with valuable information.

- **Being energetic and enthusiastic in your presentation.** There's a power that eludes most presenters – the power of attitude and enthusiasm.

- **Storytelling in a way that's relatable.** Stories must be spellbinding, enchanting, engaging, and with a POINT. And they better be your own.

- **Looking good, not put on or plastic.** Authentic is not just message, it's messenger. It's as much about being comfortable inside your skin as it is being comfortable outside your skin.

- **Being trim.** 90% of your audience is somewhere between overweight and extremely overweight. You can't be one of them and be authentic. I'm certain that many of you will read this element of authenticity and think I am dead wrong – and I'm equally certain that each of you who think I'm dead wrong is overweight.

- **Being funny.** The funnier you are, the more engaging you are, the closer the audience will listen, and the more authentic you're perceived to be. Getting the audience to laugh is tacit approval, and it's your best chance to deliver important facts. At the end of laughter is the height of listening.

- **Offering information of value.** You may not know what valuable information is, but the audience knows it the second they hear it. That's why people take notes.

- **Telling your story as it relates to the audience.** If they don't relate to or identify with your situation or your words, you lose them.

- **Being able to transfer a message.** The audience has to be able to "get it." But, more importantly, they want to learn something new that can impact their lives in a positive way. There are two important parts of this process: 1. Relevant, new information that the audience can use immediately. 2. Hope. The audience must first understand what is being said, and agree with what is being said, before they are willing to change their thinking and/or try it and apply it. Each person in the audience must say to themselves, "I get it, I agree with it, I think I can do it, I'm willing to try it."

- **Taking responsibility for the performance.** It kills me to hear a speaker tell me they had a "bad audience." Authentic is admitting you sucked.

- **Being self-confident because your message isn't some memorized drivel.** Rather, it's your authentic, meaningful material that you're presenting to your audience, and you're a world-class expert. You own your material, and you know how to personalize your message so that the audience relates.

- **Loving what you do.** If you don't love what you do, you'll be forever languishing in mediocrity. Presenting must be a passion, and your expertise must be a passion, or your talk won't be.

- **Being believable through your sincerity and passion.** It may be your 1,000th time to say it, but it's the first time the audience will hear it.

- **Being exclusive of the audience.** Do NOT use *we*, *us*, or *our* within the framework of your message. As an authentic presenter, you are not in the audience, you're in front of the audience. Using first person plural is a weak speaker's feeble attempt to gain likeability. "Look, Mary, she's just like us." Makes me puke. I have delivered more than 1,800 speeches over 15 years of speaking. I have never uttered the words *we*, *us*, or *our* ONCE. Don't have to. Don't need to. The audience is looking to you to be an inspiration, not a member – an expert, not a participant.

- **Being honorable through your actions and your kept promises.** It's not just your speech, it's your reputation. You are judged before and after your talk, not just during. Authenticity is a combination of saying, doing, and being.

AUTHENTIC IS NOT: Being self-serving, being self-indulgent, being sarcastic, being cynical, reciting a poem that you didn't write, pandering, being arrogant, looking for approval, or asking for approval.

AUTHENTIC IS NOT: Spending more time selecting what to wear than in preparing for the audience.

AUTHENTIC IS NOT: Trying to prove yourself. "I've been doing this for more than 20 years…" So what? Or, better stated, WHAT'S YOUR POINT? If it's not funny, it better be relevant to the audience.

If you can prove your claims, they will trust you, and buy from you.

You just got a testimonial...GREAT! It was from your best customer, saying how great you are. Now all you have to do is learn how to use it. A testimonial is *the* most powerful sales weapon in your sales power utility belt. And the most misused – or should I say misfired.

If you have the silver bullet, and you miss the target, no one will ever know it was a silver bullet.

NOTE WELL: The testimonial is the ONLY sales proof that you have – and the bonus is it builds trust.

When you say things about yourself, it's bragging; when someone else says it about you, it's proof. And the testimonial is the solid evidence to back up all your sales claims.

FIRST KEY QUESTION: WHEN do you use your testimonial?

SECOND KEY QUESTION: HOW do you use your testimonial?

KEY ANSWER TO BOTH: It depends. It depends on what the testimonial says, it depends where you are in the sales cycle, and it depends on the media format of the testimonial.

TESTIMONIAL LETTER: Get rid of it. "Jeffrey, what the h-e-double-l are you saying?" you whine. I'm saying that a testimonial in letter format is great to hang on a wall someplace in your office. And a quote or two excerpted for your proposal is fine. BUT the most powerful form of testimonial by far is…

TESTIMONIAL VIDEO: The modern way. The new way. And, in my opinion, the ONLY way. The video is active, alive, and believable. Video is power. Sales power. Trust power.

Ever watch an infomercial? Infomercials are FULL of testimonials. Infomercials sell product. Infomercials make money. I wonder if there's a correlation?

But there's a secret to the testimonial beyond the video – it's the CONTENT. What the testimonial "says" determines its validity AND when it should be used. The key to successful use is to time them perfectly. They are trump. Sales trump.

The biggest mistake salespeople make with testimonials is using them inappropriately. Too early is the biggest mistake.

At the wrong time is neck-and-neck. *Here's what to say and when to say it:*

To set an appointment, the testimonial must say: "I was reluctant to even set an appointment with the Acme representative, but take it from me, it was well worth my investment of time – I became, and still am, a customer."

To open a sale, the testimonial must say: "My name is Tom Jones, I'm the CEO of Acme Manufacturing. I'd like to introduce you to one of the finest young men I know."

To answer a question or overcome an objection, the testimonial must be specific. Select three questions and three objections, and get testimonials that answer and overcome.

To prove a point, the testimonial must be used at the appropriate point in your presentation.

To kill the competition, the testimonial must say, "We used to use XYZ Corp., but we switched, and we love it."

To affirm your price, the testimonial must say, "We used to use XYZ Corp, but we found that their poor quality and slow delivery actually added up costing us more money."

With a proposal, the testimonial must have three or four customers issuing a call-to-order. They tell the prospect that they were once in the same position, and they all went with Acme.

To solidify a sale, or to enhance your credibility and believability, the testimonial must say, "We've been doing business with Acme, best choice we ever made."

How do you set up the testimonial? Great question. *Just use common-sense language like:*

> **"I may not be the best person to answer that."**

> **"If they tell you what you want to hear, will you buy from me?"**

> **"Is that all you need to know before you buy?"**

> **"Let me tell you through the voice of our customers."**

> **"Can you see any reason not to buy?"**

> **"May I show you what XYZ said about the exact same thing?"**

> **"XYZ used to feel that way too, but now they're a customer – let me show you what they said."**

When you use a testimonial, you never have to brag or exaggerate again – your customers will do it for you. When you use a *video* testimonial, it's as though you were taking your best customer with you.

It's proof. It's support. It's a sale when a salesman can't make one. It's sales power. It's a video testimonial. It's trust power. Use them and take them to the bank.

Free Git✗Bit... Want more on the power of testimonials? How about a one-pager on how to get testimonials? Go to www.gitomer.com, register if you're a first-time visitor, and enter the word TESTIMONIAL in the GitBit box.

Entertain, engage, create the value, prove it, and they will buy!

I'm a salesman. I sell online training. I write about sales because I know about sales and because I make sales. Today I had two sales calls, both at the same time. One with an existing customer, and one with a prospective customer.

REAL WORLD: During every sales call – no matter where it takes place – while you are trying to qualify the customer, they are trying to qualify you. I found a strategy where I qualify myself to the customer *first*, so that they become relaxed, open, and confident about doing business with me.

REAL SALE: I arranged a meeting with a customer and a prospect, because I felt that they could do business with one another, so I brought them together at my offices for that sole purpose. Each of them could benefit from what the other sold, and each of them could sell their product to the other guy's customers.

Let me share this story about how I make sales so that you might try to make your sales the same way.

Keep in mind that this is not *how to* sell, this is how *I* sell. Big difference.

I make friends with them before I ever start to talk business.
We began the sales call with them getting to know each
other. Breakfast, open talk, laughter, sharing stories, and
finding solid common ground. I believe that friendship
is the basis for open communication. I am friendly, and I
hope that my friendliness is contagious.

I establish rapport with them by finding common ground. By
communicating conversationally, the atmosphere is relaxed
and communication is more open. The conversation is
natural, not sales-y.

I sell on my home court. More than 50 percent of my sales
appointments take place at my office, where I have total
control of the environment and all of my sales aids at my
disposal. My team is there with me if I need them, and
I have a decided advantage, having my resources at my
fingertips. It also removes any mystery from the customer
as to what they're buying, or what they're buying into.
My business personality and my human personality are
evident when I'm relaxed on my home turf.

I introduce everyone to everyone. It's important that I honor
my guests and respect my fellow workers by introducing
one to another and spending a few moments exchanging
details and pleasantries. It creates an atmosphere of
warmth and it also begins to create credibility in the minds
of the customers. They can see what they are about to buy,
and they can meet who they'll be dealing with.

I WOW! them every way I can. Every action that I take has a
WOW! factor. I execute each action the best way possible.
BEST is in everything I do.

I engage them. I talk about their business. I find out their present circumstance, their key motivators, and the core issues that are driving their current actions (or reactions). I don't probe, but I do engage. By engaging, I am able to solicit full answers and exchange meaningful data. I think here it is also fair to mention that I have studied their business before the meeting started so that I don't have to ask stupid questions. And because they already know me and feel good about me, I am able to get truthful answers and ascertain key facts. I also believe that because the meeting is taking place in my meeting room rather than theirs, they feel more open about sharing information. I can't really explain why – it just is.

I provide them tangible value. I take them into my studio and record an actual lesson that would be used in any potential training that we would agree to. The message is prepared, written, totally about their business and their issues, and drives home value points that prove I can help them. In other words, I show them what I can do for them, not tell them what I can do for them.

I prove I am different than the rest. Because my sales training company teaches buying motives rather than selling skills, because we teach customer loyalty rather than customer satisfaction, and because we stress using the voice of the customer as the basis of training, we are different from all others who stress old-world models. We do customized, personalized training that's based on a value proposition, not a system of selling, or a bunch of self-serving information.

I prove I am better than the rest. I have testimonials up the butt. I show them evidence of my company's superiority. Since we do everything in-house, I can take them into the studio and do a demo right in front of them. They can see and feel what they are about to purchase.

I help them grow their business. By bringing two people together for the purpose of doing business with each other, I created an energy in my conference room the likes of which I have rarely seen. Sparks and dollar signs were flying as they spoke of possibilities and made plans to meet again to structure a deal.

I entertain them and feed them. I find that when I am eating with someone, the conversation strays from business. And the more personal the customer is willing to be with me, the more likely I am to gain the sale. While we're talking, there's fruit and cheese. Food relaxes people.

I ask them for the sale, but only after I know they are eager to buy. The energy level at the end of the day was so high, they were selling each other on me and our capabilities. I didn't even have to ask for more business – they asked to buy. (WOW!)

BOTTOM LINE OF SALES. My customer speaks louder for my capability than I do. My customer is proof that I can support my claims.

BOTTOM LINE OF BUSINESS. I'm not always looking to make a sale – I'm looking to build a relationship, part of which is a business relationship. And sales follow. Big sales.

"I let them know I trust them, and they think of me as trustworthy in return.

I always deal truthfully with them – even if it is not to my sales advantage.

I add something of value to the relationship without any expectation of a return."

– Jeffrey Gitomer

A sales principle that leads to wealth – it's all about them.

Think about the way you sell and the way you present your product or service.

How many times do you think you use the word *we*? My bet is hundreds.

How many times SHOULD you use the word *we*? My answer is ZERO.

Everything you do or say is in "we" format, especially if you have a marketing department.

Does the customer care about you or themselves? There's an obvious answer. So why do you "we-we" all over them? They don't care about you – UNLESS you can help them.

The key in mastering any kind of sales is switching statements about you and how great you are and what you do, to statements about them, and how great they are, and how they will produce more and profit more from ownership of your product or service.

HERE'S THE SECRET: Take the word "we" and delete it. Delete it from your slides, your literature, and most especially from your sales presentations. You can use "I," but you can't use "we."

HERE'S THE POWER: When you stop using "we," you have to substitute it with the word "you" or "they" and say things in terms of the customer: how they win, how they benefit, how they produce, how they profit, how they will be served, and how they can gain peace of mind.

"We" is for selling. "You" is for buying.

MANDATE FOR UNDERSTANDING: Go through your entire presentation, record it, and listen to it actively, which means taking notes. Count the word "we." I'll bet there are PLENTY. Take out the "we," and begin to make value statements instead of selling statements.

Here's the reality in plain English:

1. **The buyer, the prospect, and the customer expect you to have knowledge of their stuff, not just your stuff.** To transfer that knowledge, the prospect needs to understand and agree with your ideas, feel your passion, feel your belief, and feel your sincerity beyond the hype of the sales pitch.

2. **You have to know their industry, not just your product.**

3. **You have to know their business, not just your product.**

4. You have to know what's new and what's next, not just your product.

5. You have to know the current trends, not just your product.

6. You have to know their marketing, not just your product.

7. You have to know their productivity, not just your product.

7.5 You have to know their profit, not just yours.

Are you getting it yet?

Here are some classic examples of "we-we thinking":

- **We have to educate the customer.** Do you really think any customer on the planet WANTS your education? I can just picture your top 25 prospects sitting around doing nothing and saying, "Boy, I sure hope those people over at Acme come over here and educate us, because we're pretty stupid."

- **You feel like you have to tell the prospect all about you, your company, and your product.** Those are three things that are guaranteed to put any prospect to sleep.

- **We offer solutions.** *Hey, Albert Einstein, do you think I'm just sitting here all day doing everything wrong, HOPING that you will come along and rescue me with your "solution?"* Solutions are an insult to a prospect. Answers are better; they're about a partnership and are relationship-driven.

- **You compare yourself to the competition, rather than differentiate from them.** You're still selling your features and benefits. More we-we. I don't want features; I want value. I don't want benefits; I want value.

- **You have a PowerPoint presentation that brags, rather than proves.** This will not put a prospect to sleep. It will put them in a DEEP sleep.

What were you thinking? Oh, you were thinking we-we.

Assuming they have a genuine need or strong desire, all you need to make a sale is:

1. Answers they need.

2. Ideas they benefit from.

3. How you differentiate from the others.

4. Value they perceive.

4.5 Trust they perceive as a result of all the other elements being in place.

And keep in mind that meanwhile the customer is qualifying you. They are forming a perception of you as you present. They are evaluating their risk of buying and doing business with you. They are formulating barriers. They are aware of their urgency of need, or not. They are doing a mental comparison between you and the others. They are thinking, and their thoughts will become your reality.

RISK REALITY: In sales, it's not what you say; it's all about how they perceive what you say. If the prospect perceives that it's all about you, then there's going to be a higher chance for unspoken risk and a lower sense of urgency on their part. If they perceive the presentation is about them, they understand it, and they need what you're offering, then their barriers and risks will be lowered or removed. This paves the path to purchase.

There's an old song titled, "Take the 'L' out of *lover* and it's OVER" from the early 1980s by a group called The Motels.

PARAPHRASE: Take "we" out of selling, or it's over. For you.

"You can trust our money back guarantee. Just send back the unused portion of our product and we'll send back the unused portion of your money!"

Managers say customer relationships are their top issue

I just read a 500-word article from some consulting firm to a Fortune 10 company on one point – "managers say that relationships are important."

Well, gohleee! Where is Gomer Pyle when you need him? Boy, what a non-surprise. Relationships are important? Now you tell me! What was I thinking all these years?

This non-information is typical of money wasted on one-dimensional consultants who tell you what you already know – but not ONE THING or ONE WORD on what to do about it.

These are the same people who think it's important to "measure" customer satisfaction. This is not just a waste of time and money. It's a total joke. It's all about customer loyalty.

There are two words that are missing from this "relationships are important" drivel that would clarify the issue while saving hundreds of thousands on consultants who have no concept of what to do and managers who continue to focus only on symptoms or desired outcomes rather than deal with real-world problems. The two words are: REAL ANSWERS.

Many companies tell me that they have *great* relationships with their customers. Many salespeople tell me that they have *great* relationships with their customers. Those *same people* lose orders on *price* to the customers they have a *great* relationship with. *What?*

COLD HARD FACT: If you lose an order to a customer because of price, then you have NO RELATIONSHIP. You're in luck! I can help both you and your customer indirectly. But let me help you first, because you don't really care about them.

In fact, you hope they never find out how oblivious they are, so you can continue to clean their clock. They can continue to blame loss of customers on price and a bunch of other wrong reasons. They'll be blaming instead of taking responsibility.

In 1998 I wrote the book, *Customer Satisfaction is WORTHLESS, Customer Loyalty is Priceless*. I didn't do it for shock; I did it for the reality of what builds a relationship: loyalty. And in order to get loyalty, you must first give it. That's the basis for a relationship. And for the record – relationships are not merely "important," they're the foundation of a strong, successful business.

Now you know what to do. Do it.

Free Git✗Bit...I have prepared an additional list of relationship ideas. To view the list, go to www.gitomer.com, register if you're a first-time visitor, and enter the words CUSTOMER WANTS in the GitBit box.

Instead of simply telling you how important the elements that will make relationships happen are (because you AND the rest of the world already know that), here, for YOUR benefit, are the actual elements:

1. **Relate to me.** Know my needs and issues. Engage me by showing me other customers who are benefiting from doing business with you.

2. **Prepare for me.** Show me that you have done your homework about my situation, not just yours.

3. **Don't waste my time.** Don't ask me what you could have found out on your own.

4. **Tell me the truth.** Truth leads to trust. I need to trust you in order to have a relationship with you.

5. **Tell me how I can use your product or service to build my business.** I want to know how I can produce in my environment.

6. **Tell me how I can profit from the relationship.** I want to know how I can profit from buying. And I want to know that you know.

7. **Show me the value, not just how it works.** What are the elements of value attached to your product or service that relate to me?

8. **Make it easy for me to do business with you.**

9. **Make service available when I need it.**

10. **Be friendly to me.** If I'm going to establish a relationship with you, I want it to be a friendly one.

11. **Respond quickly.** If I call you, it's because I need you, and I need a response now.

12. **Deliver on time.** When you tell me it's going to be there, I expect it. And it helps reinforce my feeling that you can meet my expectations.

13. **Have answers for me when I need them.** I have questions about how your product works.

14. **Stay in touch with me.** Keep me informed on a proactive basis. Make your messages more about me than you.

15. **Let me know when things or technologies change.** Keep me informed about how I can stay ahead, even if it means buying more.

16. **Keep your promises.** If you tell me something will happen, make it happen.

17. **Be a partner, not a vendor.** Tell me how we will work together. And then prove it by your deeds.

17.5 **Serve me.** I need to feel that service after the sale is more important than the emotion leading up to the order.

The relationship edge… are you on it, in it, or over it?

Beginning a relationship is easy.

Exploration is predominantly on the surface. There's nothing too deep, nothing too wide, and nothing too revealing. In the beginning, all is well. Friendships blossom. Feelings emerge. Life is good.

It's like fast dancing at a bar. You kind of get to know the other person without touching them. You watch them move, see their rhythm, exchange smiles, scream a word or two, and, at the end of the song, thank the person for their time.

You get to know the person, and decide if you want to dance again. If you like them, and believe you have some things in common, you may dance again. And again.

If you feel good about the relationship, and a bit of trust emerges, you may permit a transaction to take place – a meeting, a dinner, a sale, or, in a social setting, even a kiss.

As the relationship matures, facts and truths begin to reveal themselves, causing decisions to be made about the future of the relationship, including things like its length.

And then one day you begin to see things you've never seen before, because life takes over and reality sets in based on daily transactions and interactions, coupled with patience, emotions, feelings, and responses.

I'll refer to them as *edges*. You have *edges*, or levels, past which you will not go: tolerance levels, social levels, philosophical levels, and business levels. If someone tries to go past your edge, your tolerance level, you, in some manner, rebuff or deny them. Maybe even dismiss them.

Your compatibility for and with the other person's edges, combined with your acceptance of the other person's edges, will determine how the relationship grows or dies.

For example, I'm not a smoker. Nor am I much of a drinker. If I'm around a drinking smoker, it's past my edges, and I don't want to be around the person much. I didn't say ever. I just said much.

I may have a business relationship with a smoking drinker, but I'd never have a social relationship with him or her.

There are also ethical edges, both personal and business. If someone goes past your ethical edges, you have a reaction, often acute, that says "danger." It can be as "innocent" as cheating on their golf score or as serious as cheating on their taxes or not paying their bills, but whatever it is, it's a relationship breaker.

And then there are emotional edges – how someone reacts when something goes wrong, or how someone responds to an argument and how you feel about their reaction.

Is the person whiny? Is he quick-tempered? Is he abrasive? Is he abusive? Is he somewhat of a wildcard, flying off the handle all the time, or worse, showing characteristics that you either don't like, or fear? A temper. Hostility. Vindictiveness. Even the threat of physical violence.

In other words, is this inside (safe) or outside (unsafe) your emotional edge?

EDGES HAVE A COUNTERPOINT: Tolerance.

> You can tolerate almost anything for a short space of time. But each time someone goes over your edge, you become less and less tolerant, either verbally or silently.

Personally, I believe that "past the edge" silent thoughts are more dangerous and more powerful. They're dangerous because they're left unsaid and they allow the present situation to continue. They're more powerful because they begin to deepen and build emotion.

And, like any latent power, eventually they explode.

What are your edges? Where do you draw the line? What are you willing to accept in others in order to continue a relationship? Many spousal relationships become petty before they end – leaving the cap off the toothpaste, dirty laundry lying around, dirty dishes in the sink, the gas tank on empty – dumb little things that erode love because after a hundred abrasive times, it's over someone else's edge.

Of course, there are worse edges in personal relationships. For the purposes of this writing, I'd rather not get into them. If you've forgotten what they are, any local news program will remind you of them nightly.

Rather, I'm challenging you to widen your field of acceptable edges. Extend your patience.

Figure out how you can help first rather than complain, nag, bicker, nitpick, or whine. Figure out how you can compromise just a bit more. And figure out how you can be more of a resource than a resister, more of a yes than a no.

Your personal edges determine your business and career edges. And your happiness.

How to make a relationship of trust blossom.

When you make a sale, the first thing you do is celebrate the victory. That's okay for a minute or two, but then you have to make more sales.

What you *should* do after a sale is determine how the sale was made, and *why* the customer bought from you. This critical information will lead you to the next sale in half the time. Or less.

For years I have employed this sales law:

> If they like you, and they believe you, and they have confidence in you, and they trust you – then they may buy from you.

Customers buy because they trust you, but in order for you to gain that trust, they first had to like you AND believe you AND have confidence in you. If those elements are not present, trust (or trust enough to purchase) does not follow.

CAUTION: There's a variation of this law. In sales, trust or no trust, some customers will just take the lowest price. Avoid these people.

In business relationships, why does one person trust another person? Trust is a perception and a realization. It's based on initial feelings and perceptions by the prospective customer – value perception being a huge one. In sales, if the prospect feels value, he will begin to believe, have confidence, and *maybe* even purchase.

Relationships are based on trust – engagements and interactions over time as well as words and deeds over time. They're based on a past history of performance. Trust is not given. Trust is earned. And trust is not earned in a day – it's earned day by day.

It may take two years to earn trust, but it takes only one minute to lose it. The difference is two letters UN – truth or untruth.

Why do you trust somebody? Think about the criteria in your mind that creates permission to trust someone else. Then think of the people you trust and ask yourself *why do I trust him or her?* Reliability? Consistency? Long-term friendship? A giving person? A truthful person? An understanding person? A person whose words, thoughts, and deeds you've come to rely on and depend on in times of need? Is it someone who performs these things for you without any motive? Without any agenda? Without any expectation of something in return?

Trust is not complex. Many of the answers you come up with as to why you trust others can lead you to your own game plan for becoming trustworthy.

Here are some simple elements of trust that you must MASTER in order to make it possible for a relationship of trust to blossom:

TELL THE TRUTH. This is the number one element of trust AND relationships. Once truth has been violated, trust evaporates and may never return.

DELIVER WHAT YOU PROMISE. People hope and expect you to deliver on promises.

DO WHAT YOU SAY YOU WILL DO. This is a test for being reliable and trustworthy.

COMMUNICATE IN A TIMELY MANNER. Rapid response shows you are responsible, on top of it, and that you care.

BRING VALUE BEYOND YOUR PRODUCT OR SERVICE. What you do to help others be more successful will be a true reflection of your character.

BE ON TIME. Being on time shows you respect the other person's time. It also proves your reliability.

BE FRIENDLY. Smiling people are the gateway to open communication. It costs no extra money to be friendly.

BE SINCERE. This can only come from belief in what you do, loving what you do, and caring for others. This is not just being true to others, but being true to yourself. Sincerity comes from within.

BE APPRECIATIVE OF THEIR BUSINESS. Showing and saying genuine thanks will not only build a relationship – it will also enhance loyalty.

BE GRATEFUL FOR THE OPPORTUNITY TO BE OF SERVICE. If you have a service heart, if you love to serve others, you will build trust with every action.

BE CONSISTENT. Trust is not a once in a while thing. It's a constant thing. You can't be on time one day and late the next. You can't be friendly one day and rude the next. You can't deliver one day and not the next. I believe this element is the most difficult to master because it combines all the other elements.

GIVE TRUST. You become trustworthy by giving trust to others.

In sales, in business, and in personal relationships of all kinds, trust is THE critical element. It's the glue that binds all the other elements together. Without it, the relationship will fade, diminish, or die.

What are you doing to breed trust? What are you doing to build trust? What are you doing to enhance the trust you have built? What are you doing to guard and protect the trust you have built?

I trust you will work on it.

Here's one more idea on how to gain trust…

Write and publish your ideas, your thoughts, and your philosophy.

For the past 15 years, I've published something at least once a week. With my email magazine, it's twice a week – once on Tuesday and once on Friday in business papers. Publishing my ideas, strategies, and philosophy about sales, customer loyalty, and YES! Attitude have built trust and a loyal following of readers who have been strengthened week by week by week – 848 weeks up until now to be exact.

Consistent, value-driven actions that are published for all to see and read will build trust in the mind of the recipient even though they have never met you or seen you. My email mailing list has grown from 21,000 to more than 350,000 for one reason: People trust me enough to want to read what I have to say.

"You cannot buy trust at any price. But slowly, over time, you can build it for free."

– *Jeffrey Gitomer*

Corporate Trust

Within 10 years, corporate trust will emerge as the next big thing UNLESS corporations are stuck in the 1970s and 1980s measuring customer satisfaction instead of customer loyalty. Progressive companies that understand loyalty will seek to evolve to trust.

Loyalty comes from trust.

Major corporations are always trying to earn the trust of their employees, their customers, their shareholders, and their vendors. They do this while trying to maintain profitability and shareholder value. The balance is difficult, if not treacherous.

Oftentimes corporations will do *anything* to maintain shareholder value at the expense of customers and employees, thereby losing trust and creating low morale in the process. This is especially true in a slower economic time, or right after a merger.

The basic fundamental principles of trust and loyalty are the same. *The best way to get loyalty is give loyalty. The best way to get trust is give trust.* You can also substitute the word *earn* for the word get.

HERE'S A CLUE: In order to earn an external trusting environment, there must be an internal environment of trust. And the corporate leaders, the C-level executives, create this environment – or destroy it – with their decisions and deeds.

Enter: marketing. The surest way to make big companies look foolish. Why do I see ads telling to me to go "fly the friendly skies," and when I get there no one is friendly? The answer is that big companies spend more on their image than they do helping their employees maintain that image. And the percentage is nearly 100 to zero.

To further exacerbate the problem, JD Powers gives these same companies awards for outstanding customer *satisfaction*.

Both customers and employees are somewhere between laughing out loud and silently smirking at these "awards."

Let me get to the answers...

Trust begins the same place loyalty begins. At the top. That doesn't mean that you can't cut jobs in order to ensure profitability, but it does mean that you have to tell the truth while these circumstances are happening. And you have to tell the truth in a way that's clear. That would mean the entire truth. You have to give the people who are being let go some help and hope. The more you let people keep their dignity, the more you will earn the respect and trust of those who remain.

In order to earn trust, top-line executives must be openly communicative with their internal customers. This means being openly communicative with every employee in the company. Without this communication, rumors begin. Rumors spread ten thousand times faster than emails, and with the advent of mobile and instant text messaging, rumors become almost untraceable. Trust also breeds morale, or the decline of it.

The less communication there is, the more likely rumor will occur – and rumors create both nervousness and lack of productivity, two key elements in the fall of morale.

The executive team must be visibly engaged with other people in the company at every level. This must be done hands-on, with direct face-to-face communication. It can be done in a live speech or video messaging, both online and in podcast format.

Senior executives must also go face-to-face with customers and vendors. This ability to be directly involved not only keeps the officers current and in touch with what's really happening, it also creates incredible goodwill among employees, customers, and vendors alike.

"I need you to do a presentation on the topic of 'trust'.
If you don't have time to prepare anything,
just steal something off the Internet!"

Openness, truthfulness, and the guts to admit when things could be better are the watch-words that will breed trust, earn trust, and keep trust.

Corporations used to give employees gold watches for 50 years of loyal service. Now, in search of profit, after 23 years of service, they give pink slips.

What is the "cost" of lost trust in a corporation?

Without trust there is low morale

Without trust there is low productivity

Without trust there is poor service

Without trust there is strict policy

Without trust there is high turnover

Without trust rumors are rampant

Without trust there is no open communication

Without trust there is doubt and disappointment

I wonder if the word "trust" is used in the boardroom more often that the word "profit?" I doubt it.

People of influence are successful. Are you one of them?

Are you seeking more influence with your customers? With your boss? With your prospects? With your connections? With your associates and coworkers?

Have you ever thought about what elements go into being an influential person? Below is the list, BUT don't just read it – compare your skill levels to it, so that you can develop your understanding AND your status at the same time.

This list contains elements of the IDEAL influencer. All people of influence do not have to have all these qualities, but the more they possess, the greater their power to influence.

A power influencer is:

SMART. A person who can reason, and be reasonable. A person who can think in terms of answers, rather than fret over circumstances. Someone who sees the big picture rather than the immediate urgency.

SHREWD. Beyond smart, a shrewd person sees an answer *and* a game plan to implement it. And the implementation is seen in favor of the other, rather than in favor of himself. It doesn't mean you give up your winnings (earnings, commission), but it does mean that everyone wins, not just you.

KNOWLEDGEABLE. Beyond smart, a knowledgeable person knows what's going on in detail. Product knowledge, service knowledge, and experience. Not just how to work it, but how to use it to profit and produce.

LONG-TERM ORIENTED. Influence is determined by relationship, and relationship is preceded by long-term thinking. It's not about your quota. It's not about the end of the month. It's about doing what is best for others over an extended period of time regardless of your self-imposed deadlines.

FULL OF ANSWERS. Influencers do not always push. Often they are called upon because an answer is needed, and the caller has confidence or faith that the influencer knows the right answer *and* the best answer.

SOMEONE WITH IDEAS THAT WORK. Ideas based on past experience, the best possible answer, and a firm understanding of the circumstance will all create influence enough to be accepted and implemented.

CREATIVE. Creativity is the mother of ideas. A creative person has studied creativity and combined it with the brainpower to never be at a loss of thought in any situation.

A THINKER. Most people never spend time thinking. That's why most people are not power influencers. Thinkers are also observers. They don't just talk – they look, they think, they reason, and then they respond.

SERVICE DRIVEN, NOT SALES DRIVEN. Salespeople are only able to influence temporarily. Power influencers lead with service, and their service leads to sales.

SOMEONE WITH A GREAT REPUTATION. If you seek to become a person of influence, other people will have to corroborate your credentials and your credibility. You may think you're a person of influence, but in the end, it's not what you think; it's what others think and say about you.

SOMEONE WITH GREAT TIMING. Knows when to hold 'em. Knows when to fold 'em.

SOMEONE WITH A GREAT ATTITUDE. I don't think you can influence at the same time you're whining and complaining. And maybe you should substitute the words *power influence* with the words *positive influence.*

WELL READ. Influence comes from a combination of thinking and reasoning that's not just based on your experience. Reading will help you understand more and clarify your own thinking, even *refine* your own thinking, and it gives you an additional resource to draw from as you're building your influential base.

PUBLISHED. For the past 15 years, I have published a weekly article. That's more than 800 individual writings that have helped and influenced others in their thinking and in the actions that they take. If you seek to influence, you must do it in a multitude of formats, but I promise you that if others are influenced by your writing, they will also be influenced by the words you speak.

AN AUTHOR. A book has both influence and prestige. Articles become books. Books become read, and the people who read them will be influenced by the person who wrote them.

FRIENDLY AND WELL LIKED. All things being equal, people want to be influenced by their friends. All things being not quite so equal, people still want to be influenced by their friends. While friendly is not always the only case for influence, I believe it is the best case.

SOMEONE WHO HAS GAINED THE CUSTOMER'S (OTHER PEOPLE'S) CONFIDENCE. The more you perform, and the more successes you have, and the more wisdom you convey over time, the more confidence others will have in you. Confidence comes only as a result of performance over time.

TELLS THE TRUTH ALL THE TIME. You can temporarily influence with a lie. But once the lie is uncovered, you can never influence again.

GETS THE JOB DONE NO MATTER WHAT. People of influence are also performers. They don't just say, they DO. They walk their talk. They don't make excuses because they don't have to. They're the people who are counted on in a time of need. They are reliable and relentless. They don't leave the job until it is done.

TRUSTED. Trust is gained by combining all of these elements. But remember – it only takes one act, one lie, or one event to break trust. If you lie, trust is gone. If you quit a job in the middle, trust is gone. No one element alone builds trust, but the lack of one element can destroy it.

SUCCESSFUL. A person who has completed tasks successfully and had successful outcomes. A person who lets their record speak for him.

A WINNER. A person whose history shows he knows how to win, and he has won more often than he's lost.

NOT GREEDY. If there are givers and takers in the world, people of influence are seen as givers. People who are always thinking about or talking about money are not as influential as people who are always talking about ideas and serving others.

"A FIT." One of the most powerful but least talked about elements of relationship, trust, and influence is how comfortable people feel with each other, how easy it is to do business with each other, and how naturally the relationship is formed. You don't have to force it if it's a fit.

NOTE WELL: This list does not contain the words "has money." Having money and being influential are mutually exclusive. Maybe money gives you a slight advantage, but all the other elements outweigh it. By a ton.

It will take you years to master each element of influence. That's the good news for you, if you are dedicated to becoming a power influencer. Most other people will quit after reading this list. "Too much work," they'll say. "Not worth the effort," they'll whine.

GREAT! That means there's more room for YOU at the top.

TRUST
RECOVERY

"The only way to make a man trustworthy is to trust him."

– Henry Stimson (1867 - 1950)

General rules for trust recovery

When trust is lost, the first thing you have to do is *take responsibility*. You don't have to blame yourself or get depressed, but you better decide that you want to recover as best you can, tell the other person your intentions, and then make a long-term recovery plan.

The second thing you have to do is *come to grips with how and why the trust was violated*. Obviously some issues are lighter than others.

Most likely the higher the violation, the harder it will be to come to terms and the more likely it is that you will try to put some blame on others for your own actions.

Once you realize that you made a choice and that the violation is clearly an extension of those choices, then and only then can you *create a solid recovery plan*.

NOTE: If you continue to blame ("I did this because so and so did that…"), your recovery plan will be as feeble as your ability to take responsibility.

On the following pages are some suggested game plans for trust recovery. They're not hard and fast rules. They're simply suggestions that might help you spark a more detailed plan to recover the relationship.

Trust recovery in business.

CUSTOMERS. If the customer is still doing business with you, meet with him as fast as you can. Have some form of document that explains what you intend to do.

It may be helpful to briefly talk about what happened, but not in writing. You can apologize, but don't use the words "I'm sorry." Also do not use the words, "On behalf of…" Whatever you say to a customer or business, make certain you use the first person singular (I, me).

The tone of the meeting will pretty much determine how long recovery will take.

Be humble, ask for your customer's opinion, ask for your customer's ideas, but never ask, "What will it take for us to recover?" or "What will it take for me to recover?" You better walk in with that answer.

Maybe start by saying, "I have a couple of ideas about how our relationship might become strong again. I'd like to share them with you and get your feedback."

Whatever the customer asks you to do to recover (within reason) DO IT!

COWORKERS. Coworkers are quasi-family members. You spend as much time or more with them than you do with your real family members, and your relationship is based on the same set of family standards.

The difference is, at work, they're judging your work ethic on top of all your other ethics and actions.

> If you have committed a personal trust violation, get with the injured party one on one and talk about what happened, why it happened, how you feel about it, and what you're going to do about it.

If the violation occurred to the company (for example, you failed to complete a project on time or you committed personal acts that would cause you to lose others' trust such as making errors or being consistently late), you have to make an upper-management apology and create a new set of standards that you intend to adhere to.

Workplace trust and your success in the workplace are brother and sister. You may think it's only a small thing to talk about someone else behind their back or keep a rumor going or speak about the company or your boss in a derogatory way, but the implication of those small acts over time creates your internal reputation. For good or bad, you have chosen it and brought it on yourself. The only way to recover is to change your habits.

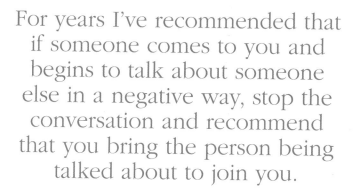

For years I've recommended that if someone comes to you and begins to talk about someone else in a negative way, stop the conversation and recommend that you bring the person being talked about to join you.

VENDORS. My dad taught me that vendors are more important than customers because there's a limited supply of vendors and an unlimited supply of customers. When a trust violation has occurred with a vendor and that vendor is a prime resource for your business, arrange a face-to-face meeting within a week of the violation. Limit your phone conversations, especially those where you're trying to make excuses for what happened.

When any kind of trust violation occurs, excuses usually fall on deaf ears, especially if the violation is a bounced check or some other financial misdeed. In order to rebuild trust with a vendor, the vendor has to have confidence in you as a customer. The good news is the vendor wants to sell you more. The bad news is you've lost your credit freedom and may have to seek a bank or other financial means to do business with that vendor.

Try to get to as high a person as you can. Try to stay away from the accounting department. And whatever you do, meet every promise that you make.

Trust recovery in life

FRIENDS. Stop for a moment and look at your history of friendship. Not the good friends – the ones who have somehow departed or disappeared.

If you were the one who violated the friendship, what could you or should you have done in order to have prevented the mistrust and preserved the friendships?

If the friend violated you, either by revealing a secret truth or creating some rumor, study how it occurred, why it occurred, and how you can prevent this in your current or future friendships.

Friendship recovery is easier than family recovery. For some reason, you can be more truthful with your friends than you can be with your family. Be truthful with your friend, and talk it all the way out. In addition, talk about the value of your friendship beyond what occurred and mutually agree that it's worth it to continue.

One of the keys to friendship is understanding how the other person's feelings can have an effect on what you say about that person.

FAMILY. There's an old song title that goes, "You always hurt the ones you love." It's a pop standard that was written in the 1940s. It talks about hurting someone close to you. The lyric of the song doesn't talk about what happened. It basically begs for forgiveness. In the real world, that's not gonna cut it.

Where your family is concerned, trust violations linger in memory for years and probably forever.

The good news is that it's your family. You love them. They love you. The bad news is that you've done something wrong, and the faster you face it, the more positive the long-term outcome will be.

Ignoring it will not make it go away. It will still be an issue for the other member or members of your family that you have hurt.

The key is TRUTH. Fess up, take responsibility, apologize, and work out a mutually agreeable resolution. It will not make the violation go away, but it will put you on the path to reconciliation and recovery.

SPOUSE. A spouse or significant other creates the most delicate trust issue because that's the person you're supposed to trust the most. In my experience, the longer a spousal relationship goes, the more secretive it becomes, when just the opposite should be true.

How many times have you heard someone in a broken marriage say, "After 15 years, we just grew apart"? You didn't share your life, or maybe you didn't share the same common interests, or maybe one partner just couldn't keep up with the other. The fact is you stopped talking about it, or you at least stopped talking about it truthfully.

And then there's lying. How do you recover from a lie, especially if you got caught? And what's worse is one lie usually leads to another.

If you wanna look at the ridiculous example of politicians caught in a lie, all of a sudden they're willing to do anything and everything to win back the public trust. And their phoniness shows through like a bad toupee.

It's no different in your marriage or cohabitation. If there's a "best way to recover," it would be to apologize before you're caught. But that takes more guts than most people have. The best way to recover from a lie is to begin telling the truth all the time even if it hurts. Omission is a lie. So the keyword would be: forthright.

The truth may hurt, but never as much as a lie.

"When I'm dieting, my doctor says it's okay to cheat once in a while. I'm going out with your friend Larry tonight."

BECOMING A TRUSTED ADVISOR

"Few things help an individual more than to place responsibility upon him and to let him know that you trust him."

– Booker T. Washington

Part One: What is Being a TRUSTED ADVISOR All About?

The truth about, and the strategies for, earning the highest accolade in the sales and business world

This section is about how to earn the position of trusted advisor in the mind of the people you associate with in business, whether they are customers, coworkers, superiors, or employees.

It's a combination of the value that others perceive in you, your actions over time, and their willingness to harmonize with and accept your advice to help them succeed.

Trust can be shown in the form of an answer, a product, a solution, a strategy, or a person that they need, or in a decision that's critical to the success of their business or career.

Trusted advisor status is about people seeking and taking your advice both as a counselor and a confidante.

People will trust you to a point where they will call at some critical stage because they know you are the ONE who can help them in a way that others cannot.

Here are some of the characteristics of a trusted advisor:

A trusted advisor always has answers or will find an answer.

A trusted advisor has a great reputation.

A trusted advisor accepts responsibility.

A trusted advisor is available.

A trusted advisor is responsive.

A trusted advisor delivers.

It's important to understand that being a trusted advisor is not simply a "responsibility" – it's an honor! You've become an authority. Your knowledge has been combined with your truth and your ethics, and you've become a respected and even needed person of value.

It's not a burden – it's a blessing. It's not something that you force on someone – it's something that must be earned. It's not a title – it's an unspoken, earned designation, and and it will lead you to more success and more fulfillment in every aspect of your business life whether in sales, service, or leadership.

Trusted advisors know no gender. There's no age barrier for a trusted advisor – and there are no restrictions.

The reason I am qualified to write this section is because I have become a trusted advisor – both in the physical presence of my customers and my coworkers, and in absence through my writings – my email magazine, my columns, and my books.

The reason I've become a trusted advisor is because my written and spoken words have become known to be valid over time. I have received thousands of emails and letters of thanks. I have changed corporate cultures. I have consistently performed over an extended period of time. And I've become known as a person who gives without the expectation of getting.

In the same way that Napoleon Hill, Dale Carnegie, Orison Swett Marden, and Earl Nightingale were trusted advisors to me, so have I become a trusted advisor to salespeople, customer service people, and business people all over the world. Maybe even to you.

Think about how much more successful you would become if the people you dealt with every day had a higher level of respect and trust for you as a person and your advice as a thinker.

CAUTION: It requires hard work.

BIGGER CAUTION: It's not something you can simply lie there and wait for. It involves thinking, reading, having a clear mind and keeping your focus on becoming a world-class expert, studying, risking, failing, having the right attitude, and lacing your boot straps tighter when times are tough.

THE COOL PART IS: You can do it. **THE COOLER PART IS:** Not many others will. **AND THE COOLEST PART IS:** Once you achieve the status, it will lead you to wealth beyond money. Not just success; fulfillment.

"I would like to be your trusted advisor. When you want reliable information about drooling, barking, licking, butt sniffing, or carpet stains, I'm your man, er dog!"

Part Two: Understanding and Self-Discovery

Understanding what it takes to become a trusted advisor and the action steps to your self-discovery

When I say "trusted advisor," what words come to mind? Relationship? Helpful advice? Strategic alliance? Consultant?

Before you begin this lesson, let me challenge you with three deep questions:

- **Do you believe you are a trusted advisor?**

- **What do you believe are the elements of business and relationships that you must master to become a trusted advisor?**

- **Do believe that your customers perceive you as a trusted advisor?**

The key to stronger relationships, sales, and loyal customers is not just the products and services you offer – the key to better relationships, more takeaways, more reorders, more sales, and more referrals is achieving the status – *earning the status* – of trusted advisor.

ACTION STEP: Take a moment to list the current accounts in which you feel you're a trusted advisor. Then list the people within those accounts who rely on you for advice and count on your trusted advisor status.

When you complete this list, the first thing to do is compare it with your entire customer base. Are you a trusted advisor to more than 20% of your customer base? Take heart. Most salespeople and managers are less than 10%. Far less.

And let me clarify before we get too deep into this concept. Being trusted and being a trusted advisor are not the same. Not even close. Being trusted is one small part in being or becoming a trusted advisor.

Consider these questions:

> **How well known is your brand?**
>
> **How respected is your brand?**
>
> **How well respected and admired is your company?**
>
> **How well respected and admired are your products and services?**
>
> **What is your company known as, and what is your company known for?**

In short, what is the character and reputation of your company and its products? How powerful is your brand?

If your company offers the best products and services and your company is trusted... then the only variable in the trust circle is YOU.

HARD QUESTION: Do you believe that you have achieved the status of trusted advisor with your customers?

I hope you do.

BUT A BIGGER QUESTION IS: What do your customers believe?

You see, it's not what YOU think you are. Rather, it's about where the customer places you in their mind. How do they see you? How do they regard you? How do they refer to you? How do they talk about you? How much do they respect you? Why do they call you? And, of course, how much do they trust you?

Here are the levels of competence you can rise to as a salesperson or a manager:

> **Salesperson**
>
> **Consultant**
>
> **Advisor**
>
> **Strategic advisor**
>
> **Trusted advisor**
>
> **Trusted advisor and resource**

NOTE WELL: These are NOT titles. They are roles you play, positions the customer regards you as. Just because your card says "Consultant" doesn't mean you are one. The proof of the title is that the customer PERCEIVES you as one.

The customer's perception of you is your reality.

THE BIGGEST QUESTIONS TO ASK YOURSELF ARE: What am I doing to earn and ensure my status of trusted advisor in the mind of the customer? What can I do to improve my relationships to strengthen that status?

Understand that becoming a trusted advisor is about much more than just having a great relationship. Trust is just the beginning. Trust is the foundation for the relationship.

I have just asked you huge questions that require personally revealing answers. These are answers you may not want to hear...maybe even answers you would rather avoid!

BUT HERE'S THE CRITICAL QUESTION: Am I doing my BEST for ALL my customers, ALL the time?

Without BEST, you will never achieve TRUST.

Here are a few action steps and reality bites to ensure greater success in your quest to earn trust and rise to the status of trusted advisor:

- **List the customers and contacts that you believe best exemplify your trusted advisor status.**

- **List the characteristics that you believe have earned you that status.**

- **List the customers that insist you attend their decision making meetings.**

And finally...

- **List three elements, strategies, or skills that you believe would help elevate your trusted advisor status, and make appointments with yourself to work on these areas.** Concentrate especially on those elements that can help you gain access to more decision-making meetings.

The value of achieving trusted advisor status is that you go from the outside as a vendor to the inside as a partner.

- **A trusted advisor, not a bidder.**

- **A valued resource, not a presenter.**

- **A productivity expert, not a product regurgitator.**

- **A profit producer, not a price seller.**

A trusted advisor is not someone waiting in the lobby to make a presentation. A trusted advisor is someone who is sought after and welcomed into the inner circle.

Part Three: The Elements and Characteristics of Trusted Advisors

What are the elements of a trusted advisor?

CAUTION: These elements are as tough to achieve as they are strategic to your success.

- **Trusted advisors are value providers, not suppliers or vendors.**

- **Trusted advisors concentrate on business building, not just business seeking, and they build on behalf of the customer.**

- **Trusted advisors are considered friends by their customers.**

- **Trusted advisors are liked, believed, respected, and trusted.**

- **Trusted advisors provide information that is valuable to the customer.**

- **Trusted advisors are able to combine trust and valuable information.**

- **Trusted advisors understand the situation their customers are in, and they're willing to risk being right to do what's best for the customer.**

- **Trusted advisors are empowered by their customers to act, and they're willing to take that action.**

- **Trusted advisors help customers profit, not just save money.**

- **Trusted advisors figure out a way to get more face time.**

- **Trusted advisors make decisions based on the relationship, not the quarter or the quota.**

- **Trusted advisors are always invited into the classrooms and the boardrooms. They are invited into the classroom to help facilitate learning, and they are invited into the boardroom to help make the right decisions.**

A trusted advisor displays professionalism, friendliness, competence, product knowledge, and expertise – not just as an expert, but also as an expert communicator.

REALITY: These elements are the BARE MINIMUM – they are the basics that qualify you to earn the title of trusted advisor.

To earn the status of trusted advisor, these basics must be *combined* with your knowledge of the customer's business, and how the customer uses, produces, benefits from, and profits from your products and services. You also need to know how the customer *values* you and *trusts* you to make those things happen.

MAJOR CLUE: The customer must PERCEIVE that you have these qualifications, or you will allow your competition to get in the door and establish some sort of position.

Trusted advisors keep competitors at bay. And they bridge the gap from a satisfied customer to a loyal customer.

Remember the list I asked you to make at the beginning of the first lesson? For those of you who actually did it, I wonder if you still have the same people on the list? And for those of you who did not make a list – I would imagine that after you've read this information, there are fewer people on the "they consider me a trusted advisor" list than you were thinking.

"They're special glasses that help you see yourself the way others see you!"

Trusted Advisor Self-Evaluation

This self-evaluation will help you gain a clearer idea of what you must do to establish your position, your relationship, and your reputation...

1=poor 2=average 3=good 4=very good 5=excellent
1=never 2=hardly ever 3=sometimes 4=frequently 5=always

❐ I'm a value provider, not a supplier or vendor.

1 2 3 4 5

❐ I concentrate on business building – not just business seeking – and I build on behalf of the customer.

1 2 3 4 5

❐ I am considered a friend by my customers.

1 2 3 4 5

❐ I am liked, believed, respected, and trusted.

1 2 3 4 5

❐ I provide information that is valuable to my customers.

1 2 3 4 5

❐ I am able to combine trust and valuable information.

1 2 3 4 5

❐ I understand the situations my customers are in, and I'm willing to risk being right.

1 2 3 4 5

❐ I am empowered by my customers to act, and I'm willing to take action.

1 2 3 4 5

❐ I help customers profit, not just save money.

1 2 3 4 5

❐ I figure out a way to get more face time.

1 2 3 4 5

❐ I make decisions based on the relationship, not the quarter or the quota.

1 2 3 4 5

❐ I am always invited into the classrooms and the boardrooms of the customer.

1 2 3 4 5

❐ I am invited into the classroom to help facilitate learning.

1 2 3 4 5

❐ I am invited into the boardroom to help my customers make the right decisions and the best decisions.

1 2 3 4 5

Scoring is simple – go back and check the boxes where you scored a 1, 2, or 3. Those are your weak areas. This self-evaluation becomes your personalized, customized game plan that shows you where you need to improve.

Part Four: Think about WHO and WHY

If they like you, believe you, have confidence in you, and trust you, then they MAY buy from you. Liking you leads to trusting you.

Think about your three
most trusted advisors.
I bet you like all
of them. Some of them
you may even love.

Now that you have an understanding of what it means to be a trusted advisor – and you're clear on the elements that will earn you the status – it's time to make a game plan and take action so that you can become proficient at earning the status of trusted advisor.

First – list your ten best contacts: your own Top Ten. These are the ones that have the most value, and the ones you want to be certain you will reach that level of trusted advisor with.

Then – list a few other contacts that you'd like to gain trusted advisor status with.

Next to each of the contacts you listed, write your answers to the following 4.5 questions:

1. What steps are you taking to bring value to this customer?
Make a list of them.

2. What ideas are you generating on the customer's behalf?
List the best ones in the past three months.

3. How are you increasing the customer's productivity? Write
a paragraph of actual happenings.

4. How much PROFIT did you put on the table? NOTE WELL:
I did not say *savings*. What have you done to make the customer money? Better stated, how did you or your products earn the customer money?

4.5 How well did your ideas perform? How well did your advice and consulting pay off?

NOTE: I am not trying to be your mother or your father or your boss – I'm trying to help you build relationships to a level where contract renewals are a certainty based on value, and loyal relationships endure based on perceived value and trust. This isn't about pointing the finger. It's about the value you provide – and the trust that you have earned.

These 4.5 questions are the heart and soul of becoming a trusted advisor. The hardest part of the process is to answer these questions truthfully, recognizing your own gaps between where you are and where you need to be, and then working at mastery every day.

Part Five: The POWER of Engagement

Trusted advisors take action. Another word for action is WORK. Begin taking trusted advisor actions.

In order to become proficient at the designation of trusted advisor, you must be engaging.

> Trusted advisors **ENGAGE** by finding common ground – things you share mutual interest in.

> Trusted advisors **ENGAGE** by peaking interest with questions.

> Trusted advisors **ENGAGE** by knowing how *the customer* wins.

> Trusted advisors **ENGAGE** by stating their price with confidence and adding the quote, "Mr. Jones, our prices are fair and firm."

In my experience, I've found that salespeople who discount their price create a double lack of belief. The customer believes in it less, and the salesperson believes in it less.

How does what you're saying impact the customer in a positive way? Where's the value? Where's the profit? Does the customer honestly feel that YOU are worth the price?

"If customers seem interested, part of the reason is that you are interesting. Trusted advisors ENGAGE by being interesting – and value based."

– Jeffrey Gitomer

Part Six: You Must Become Proficient Before You Can Master. There is No Substitute for HARD WORK.

HERE'S YOUR PROFICIENCY GAME PLAN: You must call on – visit – three to five important customers or important contacts every week and execute at least one of the trusted advisor actions. Bring an idea, offer something to help them produce more, something that brings them value, or something that earns them profit. In short, something that builds trust.

Talk to them over breakfast or lunch. Build the rapport that leads to relationships. Build trust that helps you uncover real issues and real needs.

Trusted advisors know it's not just your products and services. If you sell software, it's all about how the software is used, and how the power of the hardware is maximized. Trusted advisors know that the safety and security of data is always a top-of-mind issue for customers. They know that productivity and profit are equally important.

And it's the SAME for any product or service. Yours included.

Part of your game plan must also be to send a value message to every top contact or connection every week. And if you're sending a value message, like a value-based email, or the best idea of the week, then why aren't you sending it to all your customers?

To become proficient at the designation of trusted advisor, you must also be involved in the community. Are you visible in the community *and* in the business community? Not just a leader in your company – I'm talking about YOU becoming a community leader or a volunteer by helping others less fortunate than you.

The challenge is to balance your time. Lean toward your personal success first, and be careful not to dedicate time you don't have. Good first steps are charities or groups involving housing, child assistance, better health, or a noble environmental cause.

Be patient. It may take a year to become proficient. The good news is that during that time you will also form success habits that will last a lifetime.

HERE'S THE SECRET: I have just laid out a game plan that will work – IF you are willing to work at it. You can be on the road to becoming a trusted advisor at the highest level, IF you do the HARD WORK to get yourself there.

Here's the best part of becoming a trusted advisor – sales are easy. People will buy – not just from your company, but from YOU. The paradox of doing the work it takes to become a trusted advisor is that most salespeople are not willing to do the hard work it takes to make selling easy.

Please don't let that person be you.

I'm about to reveal the most powerful element of becoming a trusted advisor – but not until you have become proficient at the process. This means scheduling more face-to-face meetings and practicing every element until you feel you own it.

When you feel you're ready for the next lesson, go for it!

"Who are you going to believe, a knowledgeable, trained sales professional like me? Or a bunch of miserable whiners who have nothing better to do than waste their lives complaining about little things like customer service and product safety?"

Part Seven: Upon Arrival, Make Certain Your Seatbelt is Fastened…

In Part Six, I said that becoming a trusted advisor is attainable – "IF you do the HARD WORK to get yourself there." I've been saying throughout that most people are not willing to do the hard work that makes selling easy.

What it means is that the higher level of trusted advisor you achieve, the easier sales become. The hard work is in first attaining the status.

Make sure the actions you take are in the best long-term interest of the customer, not just the short-term actions of a sales quota. Your customers are counting on your advice to help them produce and profit.

The reason salespeople take short-term, sales-oriented actions, is because their pipeline is empty – hardly a situation for a trusted advisor now, is it?

Mastery at becoming a trusted advisor comes only after you have become proficient. You have not only mastered the trusted advisor actions, but you take those actions consistently.

A huge part of being a trusted advisor is your reliability and your consistency. Those elements lead to becoming the ONE person your customers count on when they need an answer.

Mastery does not mean perfection. It does mean that you have achieved the highest HUMAN level of excellence.

Everyone makes mistakes – the questions are *how do you take responsibility for them, and not blame others for them? How do you take steps to ensure that you have both learned the lesson – and will not repeat it?*

The elements of mastery are the same as proficiency... except for one. The customer has to like you, believe you, have confidence in you, and trust you. And you have to have enough confidence in yourself to give up control of conversations and situations and still prevail.

As a trusted advisor, you must make sure there's a fit between your products and services and the customer's true needs and values. Trusted advisors have mastered this critical element.

Trusted advisors NEVER have to justify their existence to customers. They have proven themselves beyond question and have earned loyalty.

Salespeople are always trying to qualify the customer – trusted advisors know that the customer is qualifying them.

Trusted advisors never go into a sale or a renewal with the fear of loss. They enter with ideas, value, answers, and with a desire to gain for the customer, for their company, and for themselves.

Trusted advisors at the mastery level realize that understanding is a two-way street. They have to understand the customer – and the customer has to understand them!

Here are a few more mastery ideas and strategies:

- **Communicate as you would to your best friend.**

- **Modify your time between seriousness and humor.**

- **Be yourself at all times – because you have to come back, and it's very hard to remember who you used to be in the last conversation.**

- **Be positive, both in knowledge and help.**

- **Relax. Trusted advisors aren't panicked since they have answers.**

Those who have reached mastery know that "trusted advisor" is not a title or a name you give yourself; it's EARNED through your words, actions, and deeds.

There are two tests that will reveal your level of trusted advisor status.

The first test is the "*Drop-In test*." Can you drop in and be seen? I've created a mini-lesson about dropping in that you can take at your leisure.

The second test, and the one key measurement of your status as trusted advisor, is when they call you. The customer calls because they believe you have the answer or can solve their problem. Or the customer calls because they know you're the BEST ONE to help them. That's a status that money can't buy – *but hard work can*.

And when they call, it's the beginning of a referral. Your customer is willing to recommend you to others because they trust that you will do the same in other relationships that you did for them.

Free Git✗Bit...To take the tests, go to www.gitomer.com, register if you're a first-time visitor, and enter the words TRUSTED ADVISOR TEST in the GitBit box.

It's the highest level of excellence for your customer, reputation for your company, and fulfillment for you.

Trusted advisor is an achieved status – and the people who get there have undergone the most rigorous skill test and personal development test of their career.

TRUTH, TRUST, VALUE

"As soon as you trust yourself, you will know how to live."

– Johann Wolfgang von Goethe (1749 - 1832), Faust

The Value of Trust

Can you think of words that define the value of trust?

Valuable? Worth a fortune? Golden?

Priceless is the only word that really describes it. Trust has immense, immeasurable value. And when you put the words "don't" or "I don't" in front of trust, all of that value is lost.

"I don't trust those people."

"I don't trust my boss."

"I don't trust that guy."

"I don't trust my husband anymore."

"I don't trust those kids."

"I don't trust MY kids."

Vocalized distrust is not only disheartening; it also reinforces the feeling and the thought. Trust has power either way. Whether you have it, or have lost it.

Rumored distrust is more damaging. It's talking about people behind their back, or people talking about you. Even if it's not true, the damage is done when the words are spoken.

There are values placed on trust and in trust that apply to every aspect of your life.

Here they are for you to ponder and capitalize on:

THE VALUE OF TRUST AT WORK. Allows you to take on responsibility and grow. You become the go-to person.

THE VALUE OF TRUST IN YOUR EVERYDAY BUSINESS DEALINGS. Allows you to complete transactions, make sales, and build relationships.

THE VALUE OF TRUST IN YOUR EVERYDAY PERSONAL DEALINGS. Allows you to gain a powerful reputation as a person of value.

THE VALUE OF TRUST WITH YOUR FRIENDS. Friendship is at the core of all relationships. You can usually count your true friends on one hand. Trust cannot be asked for, only earned. Trust cannot be measured, only valued.

THE VALUE OF TRUST WITH YOUR EXTENDED FAMILY. Relatives are family. At holidays and special occasions, they're the ones you celebrate with. Celebrate the value of their trust in you.

THE VALUE OF TRUST WITH YOUR PARENTS AND SIBLINGS. Most people lie to their parents more than anyone else combined. "I didn't want to hurt their feelings," is the lie you tell yourself. More than anyone else, you need your family for love and support. Earn it, don't ask for it or demand it.

THE VALUE OF TRUST WITH YOUR SPOUSE OR SIGNIFICANT OTHER. Open dialog and deepened feelings based on truth and trust, not just trust. Having faith in the other person and having their best interest at heart at all times.

THE VALUE OF TRUST WITH YOUR KIDS. If you want to have influence in their choices and their success, if you want their love and respect, then trust is a vital aspect of your ability to communicate successfully.

THE VALUE OF TRUST TO YOURSELF. I stated at the beginning or the book, that you can't trust others until you trust yourself. Trust in yourself is what makes all other trust happen and blossom.

> Invest your lifetime building trust. The value will exceed the work you put forth. Spend not a minute putting trust in jeopardy. It's far too painful to overcome or rebuild the loss.

Trust that you have the capacity to believe in yourself, and the strength and courage to transfer those thoughts and beliefs in the form of trust to others. Your life will be better when you do.

The truth about truth.
No truth, no nothing.

For years, hotel bathrooms have been asking me to "Save the Planet." There are hanging signs asking me to use my towels several times so that "millions of gallons of water" can be saved and the earth's ecosystem can be realigned.

NOW I ASK YOU: Does that hotel want to save the planet or a few bucks? Who thinks "planet?" Who thinks "a few bucks?" Why can't they just be honest and tell me that I can reduce their operating costs a bit if I reduce my towel usage, and it's also good for the environment? Why can't they just be honest with me?

I photographed a business sign I saw in a shopping center parking lot in Coos Bay, Oregon. It read, "We can't change the world, but we can change your oil." That business was booming, and its customers were smiling.

Mission statements mean nothing. Companies tell you how great they want to become and how great they want to treat their customers – and then they treat their people with disrespect. Most CEOs can't recite their company mission statement.

Giant corporations and their accounting firms have gone bankrupt because they lied, omitted, shredded, or manipulated the truth. And many of their CEOs are in jail for lying and cheating.

Airlines? I don't need to go into an explanation, that's how pathetic their "truth" has become.

Politicians? Ditto. Actually they're WORSE than airlines, and maybe the worst of the worst, the lowest of the low. When I ask my audiences, "How many of you think that all politicians lie?" EVERY HAND GOES UP. Is that sad, or what?

Former president Bill Clinton lied about sex. You probably have, too. All the other liars in Congress got together and wanted to throw him out of office for lying. Hello!

Other politicians – at all levels – when called to tell the truth suddenly lose their memory of what happened. Or worse, they invoke the Fifth Amendment, and choose not to incriminate themselves. It's another form of lying – withholding truth.

It's interesting that these same lying politicians pass laws compelling others to tell the truth or face consequences. The Truth-in-Lending law has helped consumers immensely. Sad that such a law has to be written. You would think that the people responsible for lending would just be honest.

Honesty is a scary sales word. Truth is a scary word. People fear having to face these words. I know I have.

And just so we understand each other, I'm no perfect example of piety – far from it. Many of the lessons and examples set here are from the music I had to face from my own forms of untruth.

And just so we're on the same page about truth and lies:

"Omission" is a lie.

"For their own good" is a lie.

"Didn't want to hurt them" is a lie.

"Small lie" is a lie.

"Hiding facts" is a lie.

Any questions? It's one of the Ten Commandments, yet men of the cloth lie. Telling the whole truth takes character, conviction, and courage. Telling the whole truth takes ethics, morality, honesty, and full disclosure.

That doesn't seem hard on the surface, but apparently no one these days is willing to walk a mile to return a penny. That's how President Lincoln got the nickname, "Honest Abe." You'll never hear anyone say, "Honest Bill" or "Honest George." They have other nicknames attached to their virtues.

There's an old saying that goes, "How can you tell when a salesman is lying?" Answer: "His lips are moving." That does not speak well for the reputation of salespeople.

Every salesperson, every company, seeks to build relationships with its customers. At the apex is truth. It's how to keep relationships together, and why they fall apart.

No truth, no trust.

The lack of truth makes trust fall apart. Once you lie and someone catches you or even thinks it, you will spend an eternity trying to regain trust. At home or at work – maybe especially at home.

When people say, "I've lost my trust in you" or "I've lost my faith in you," it's because they doubt your ability to tell the truth. They will say, "I can't believe a word you say," because they have caught you lying before and believe you'll do it again.

If you want to understand the power of truth and lies and what they can mean to a person's career and a person's life, then think about truth as it relates to Pete Rose, Roger Clemens, Barry Bonds, and Mark McGwire. Strike three.

"Of course you can trust me. If I was lying, I'd have my fingers crossed!"

You don't "get" respect, you "earn" it

In 1978, Rodney Dangerfield burst onto the comedy scene claiming he "got no respect." That theme earned him millions of laughs and millions of dollars. The reason is that it connected with his audience, many of whom also got no respect – no respect from their employer, family, or customers. Rodney was their champion, their antihero.

How respected are you? How respectful are you? How well do you believe you command the respect of others?

Respect is intangible. It's a feeling, and it's an earned position. Contrary to popular belief, bosses do not *command* respect, they *earn* respect. And bosses who do not earn the respect of their people have a high employee turnover rate and then can only stand around and wonder why.

Respect is earned by words and by actions. Things like keeping your promises, proactively providing service, becoming more personally involved with the success of your customer, and taking responsibility when the responsibility is not really yours earn you respect.

It's the extra effort. It's the extra mile. It's the extra measure of sincere effort that you put into your dialogue or your process. Others can sense that you care about them and will respect that effort.

Very few people will actually say, "I respect you." Rather, they will do things that prove their respect without ever having to say the word. Things like placing an order, placing a second order, or giving you a referral all prove that you have earned a customer's respect. Even things like taking your phone call or returning your phone call show respect.

One of the keys to respect is the word *personal.* How personal are you in your actions? How personal are you in your communication? The more personal you are with others, the more respect you will earn.

But there is a secret to respect. If you master this secret, you will be able to create a respectful atmosphere in any environment you encounter.

THE SECRET IS: In order to earn the respect of others, you must first respect yourself.

This means you have to have confidence in yourself. You have to like what you do. You have to be willing to serve. You have to like yourself, and you have to love yourself. Like and love are two separate issues. You may like yourself for how you look, or how you sell, or how you communicate, but you love yourself for who you are, what you believe in, and what or who you seek to become.

Loving yourself gives you the ultimate opportunity to respect yourself. I'm not saying that you have to be a goody two-shoes – I'm certainly not, and I have a TON of respect for myself.

What it means is *doing the right things* for yourself, *taking the right actions* for yourself, and loving yourself enough that it's evident when you enter a room – evident that your expressions come as much from your heart as they do from your mind, and the same with your actions.

I challenge you to spend one day in retrospect. Take a flip chart and begin to document all the good things that you've done for yourself and all the good things that you've done for others. Be real enough with yourself to admit what you like about yourself and what you love about yourself.

Then document what you need to change about yourself that will make you better and stronger. Maybe your self-respect suffers from the way you see yourself in the mirror, or some of the personal choices that you make, or maybe it's your environment. But whatever it is, if you don't acknowledge it, you will never be able to change it or enhance it. You'll never be able to grow in earning your respect from others until you grow in respecting yourself.

One of the most interesting parts of respect is that there's no measuring tool; there's no "How much do you respect me?" Respect begins with an opportunity and ends with reality. You can only get it by earning it, and it can only grow slowly over time.

Free Git✗Bit...For a bit more on the secret elements of self-respect, go to www.gitomer.com, register if you're a first-time visitor, and enter the word RESPECT in the GitBit box.

"The secret is easy – *do the right thing all the time*, and respect will be yours. Say the right words, take the right actions, and believe in your heart that it's the best you can do – for yourself first, and for others second."

– Jeffrey Gitomer

Thank YOU for being my customer!

Books, my books included, usually end with thanks to a bunch of people who the reader has no connection with.

This book is a little different.

The biggest thank you I can issue and the biggest debt of gratitude that I have is to YOU – my reader, my supporter, my customer, and my unknown friend.

Words cannot express the feelings I experience every time an email arrives thanking me for how much I've helped someone or when some package arrives with a baseball card, a pin, or a book that someone, through a random act of kindness, gave to me because they felt that through my writing I have given so much to them.

For that reason, the final acknowledgment of this book and the final statement of thanks go to you – with appreciation and respect.

Photograph by Yanick Déry

**Jeffrey delivering his Speakers
Hall of Fame acceptance speech.**

Jeffrey Gitomer
Chief Executive Salesman

AUTHOR. Jeffrey Gitomer is the author of *The New York Times* best sellers *The Sales Bible, The Little Red Book of Selling, The Little Black Book of Connections*, and *The Little Gold Book of YES! Attitude*. All of his books have been number one best sellers on Amazon.com, including *Customer Satisfaction is Worthless, Customer Loyalty is Priceless, The Patterson Principles of Selling, The Little Red Book of Sales Answers*, and his latest best-selling book *The Little Green Book of Getting Your Way*. Jeffrey's books have sold millions of copies worldwide.

OVER 100 PRESENTATIONS A YEAR. Jeffrey gives public and corporate seminars, runs annual sales meetings, and conducts live and Internet training programs on selling, customer loyalty, and personal development.

BIG CORPORATE CUSTOMERS. Jeffrey's customers include Coca-Cola, D.R. Horton, Caterpillar, BMW, Cingular Wireless, MacGregor Golf, Ferguson Enterprises, Kimpton Hotels, Hilton, Enterprise Rent-A-Car, AmeriPride, NCR, Stewart Title, Comcast Cable, Time Warner Cable, Liberty Mutual Insurance, Principal Financial Group, Wells Fargo Bank, Baptist Health Care, BlueCross BlueShield, Carlsberg, Wausau Insurance, Northwestern Mutual, MetLife, Sports Authority, GlaxoSmithKline, AC Neilsen, IBM, The New York Post, and hundreds of others.

IN FRONT OF MILLIONS OF READERS EVERY WEEK. Jeffrey's syndicated column "Sales Moves" appears in business journals and newspapers in the United States and Europe; and is read by more than four million people every week.

ON THE INTERNET. Jeffrey's WOW! websites, www.gitomer. com and www.trainone.com, get more than 100,000 hits per week from readers and seminar attendees. His state-of-the-art presence on the web and e-commerce ability has set the standard among peers, and has won huge praise and acceptance from his customers.

TRAINONE ONLINE SALES TRAINING. Online sales training lessons are available at www.trainone.com. The content is pure Jeffrey – fun, pragmatic, real world – and can be immediately implemented. TrainOne's innovation is leading the way in the field of customized e-learning.

SALES CAFFEINE. Jeffrey's weekly e-zine, *Sales Caffeine*, is a sales wake-up call delivered every Tuesday morning to more than 350,000 subscribers, free of charge. *Sales Caffeine* allows Jeffrey to communicate valuable sales information, strategies, and answers to sales professionals on a timely basis. To sign up, or for more information, visit www.salescaffeine.com.

SALES ASSESSMENT ONLINE. The world's first customized sales assessment, renamed a "successment," will not only judge your selling skill level in 12 critical areas of sales knowledge, it will also give you a diagnostic report that includes 50 mini sales lessons. This amazing sales tool rates your sales abilities and explains your customized opportunities for sales knowledge growth. This program is aptly named *KnowSuccess* because you can't know success until you know yourself.

AWARD FOR PRESENTATION EXCELLENCE. In 1997, Jeffrey was awarded the designation of Certified Speaking Professional (CSP) by the National Speakers Association. The CSP award has been given fewer than 500 times in the past 25 years and is the association's highest earned award.

SPEAKER'S HALL OF FAME. In 2008, Jeffrey was elected by his peers to the Speaker's Hall of Fame. The designation, CPAE (Counsel of Peers Award for Excellence), honors professional speakers that have reached the top echelon of performance excellence.

Buy Gitomer, Inc.

310 Arlington Avenue Loft 329 • Charlotte, North Carolina 28203
704/333-1112 • www.gitomer.com

Other titles by Jeffrey Gitomer

THE SALES BIBLE, NEW EDITION
(Harper Collins, 2008)

THE LITTLE PLATINUM BOOK OF CHA-CHING!
(FT Press, 2007)

THE LITTLE GREEN BOOK OF GETTING YOUR WAY
(FT Press, 2007)

THE LITTLE GOLD BOOK OF YES! ATTITUDE
(FT Press, 2007)

THE LITTLE BLACK BOOK OF CONNECTIONS
(Bard Press, 2006)

THE LITTLE RED BOOK OF SALES ANSWERS
(FT Press, 2006)

THE LITTLE RED BOOK OF SELLING
(Bard Press, 2004)

CUSTOMER SATISFACTION IS WORTHLESS, CUSTOMER LOYALTY IS PRICELESS
(Bard Press, 1998)

Several of Jeffrey's books
are now available in
audio and video format.

You can listen, read, and watch!

To purchase your own copies,
visit www.gitomer.com
or your favorite bookseller.